THE GOLDEN BALL AND THE GOLDEN STRING

1st Edition
published in 2011 by

Woodfield Publishing Ltd
Bognor Regis PO21 5EL England
www.woodfieldpublishing.co.uk

ISBN 1-84683-112-1

Printed and bound in England

The cover picture, by the author, depicts Bireh, a Moslem village adjoining the Christian village of Ramallah. Tradition says that somewhere near here Mary and Joseph turned back to look for the boy Jesus in Jerusalem.

The Golden Ball
and the
Golden String

*Memories of Life and Work
in the Middle East 1939-1945*

EILEEN ELIZABETH GIDNEY

Woodfield

Woodfield Publishing Ltd

Bognor Regis ~ West Sussex ~ England ~ PO21 5EL

tel 01243 821234 ~ **e/m** info@woodfieldpublishing.co.uk

Interesting and informative books on a variety of subjects

For full details of all our published titles, visit our website at
www.woodfieldpublishing.co.uk

"Golden Balls" from timeless friends

I give you the end of a golden string,
Only wind it into a ball
It will lead you in at Heaven's gate,
Built in Jerusalem's wall.

William Blake

The most beautiful experience we can appreciate
is the sensation of the mystical –
he to whom the emotion is a stranger,
who can no longer wonder and stand in awe,
is as good as dead.

Albert Einstein

Grant me –
Eternal use of these, my ink and palette,
And every day thou shalt receive my writings,
And thou shalt find that I have written truly

**Translation from an ancient Egyptian poem,
written about 3,000 B.C.**

Good Lord –
Invigorate my memory
Give light to my reason
Inspire my mind
Fructify all my understanding
And let my heart leap with joy

From a prayer of Queen Elizabeth 1

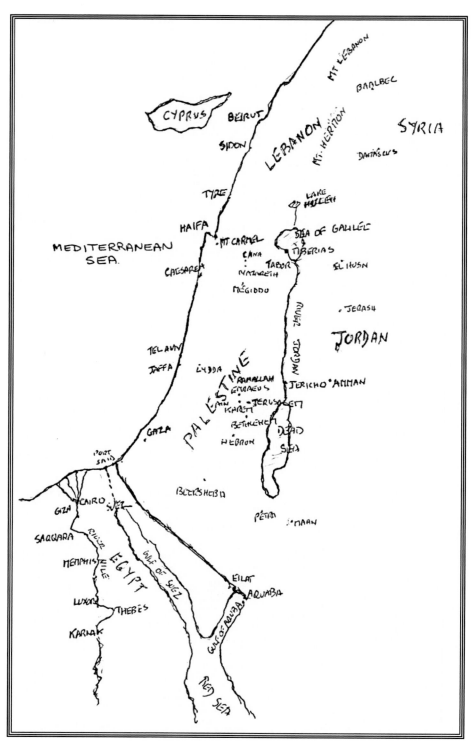

Author's sketch map of places visited.

~ CONTENTS ~

Preface

Dear Readers,

This is an amateur book. I hope you will find something to enjoy in it. On re-reading it, I find I have a combined scrapbook, snapshot album and some fragments of an anthology. There is a certain continuity, but most chapters are complete in themselves and could be read in any order. I suggest you select what you think might interest you and scrap the rest.

I wish you restful reading and many happy days and happy memories of your own to take into old age.

Yours, in friendship,

Introduction

These recollections were written for my friends, at the suggestion of some of them; they are extensions of conversations that occurred from time to time.

As I wrote, I had in mind three groups of friends: those who themselves had lived in the Holy Land as I did, or who had visited it; those who wish they had done so, and those who hope to go there in the future. The first group, on reading what I have written, will have their own memories stirred. For the second group, indeed for every reader, I have tried to give vivid impressions to share with me. For the last group, contemplating a visit, I have sought to give accurate information, checking wherever possible, to help them on their way and to make sure that they know before going just what they do not want to miss. If this falls into the hands of anyone outside these groups, it will probably be just a minor fragment of social history.

There are two themes behind my writing: firstly, I wanted to show how different teaching overseas can be from teaching in Britain, when you enter into the life of a different country and different peoples. Secondly, after reading a book about the Mandate years, heavily weighted with politics, I wanted to write about the ordinary life which mainly prevailed, especially during the wartime years of 1939-45.

"I have written truly" said the ancient Egyptian whose words I have quoted elsewhere. I have tried to write truly, but after nearly 60 years, factual truth can be elusive! Memory plays one tricks. On re-reading my letters from Palestine, which I found my parents had kept, I discovered that where I thought I had been accompanied by two people, I had been with three; somewhere in time I had lost one! Using my letters as a guide, I have been able to verify a number of happenings. I hope you will agree with me that there is a truth of experience, something that transcends facts and approaches "the sensation of the mystical". In this sense, I trust I have "written truly".

Before I began to write, I put on my rose-coloured spectacles – "Rosy Crystal". Not every moment of more than six years away from home can be happy, but I never regretted my decision to go to Jerusalem. They were golden years: I cherish the friendships I made with many different people and the experiences I was privileged to enjoy. I threw my golden ball and it went in the right direction.

❖ ❖ ❖

1. The Ball Rolls: Going to Jerusalem

Whither away, fair rover, and what thy quest?
   A Passer-by – Robert Bridges

One day drifts to another
Time is not – only the starred night
And freshblown day are true
One day on a ship is much like another
   Shipboard – Cecilia Jones

Were you ever given a ball when you were very young? Of course you were; we all liked playing ball. Have your ever woven a ball? In my later life, I have been interested in the art of needle and thread and I have seen how fascinating balls can be made with silken threads of many colours and overlaid with strands of gold and silver. Before I discovered Blake's poem, I had thought of the symbolism balls could have; each of us is a little speck on a great globe; balls are natural to us. We are each given the threads of opportunity and decision to weave a life; or perhaps we weave a ball of our dreams and then throw it to see where it runs and which dreams come true. In 1939 I threw my golden ball. It rolled across the globe – to Jerusalem.

I had graduated in English Language and Literature at Liverpool University in 1938 and then spent a year gaining a Diploma in Education. That last year, I was also very busy as joint President of the Guild of Undergraduates (Students' Union); a very rewarding year, but overshadowed by the war-clouds gathering; we sometimes wondered what our future would be. Guy Fletcher, my co-President, and I were asked by the authorities to make known through the Guild how to join the forces, and it also fell to me to make welcome newly-arrived refugee Jewish students who were already leaving Germany. Carefree days were over; we were entering the real world.

Should I volunteer to become a WREN, a WAAF, or an AT? Square-bashing did not appeal to me, but other aspects of service life I felt I could cope with, and working with all sorts of people in a community I knew I could enjoy. But the string in my ball that kept on glinting at me said "You have always wanted to teach English". My motives, I suppose were somewhat mixed, as I now think motives often are. I wanted to serve, yes; I wanted to relieve my parents of providing for me; I wanted to be independent and make my own life; I wanted to travel, not just holiday travel; I wanted to see how other people lived, to share their life; I wanted the whole cake, not just an annual fortnight's nibble. I wanted a congenial job which I could do successfully.

During my last years at University, I had got to know Bishop Gresford Jones, Bishop of Warrington, and his wife, who had been very kind to me. They perhaps led my thoughts towards teaching overseas; this and the scramble for jobs that was going on at home influenced me. There was considerable graduate unemployment and a number of people were being forced to turn in other directions.

Soon, I was considering going to India. Then one day, as I scoured the Educational Times, I spotted an advertisement for an English Mistress at the Jerusalem Girls' College. Jerusalem! Beginning from Jerusalem; then India perhaps, Rome, Greece, Egypt, China – all those wonderful ancient civilisations! The golden ball was rolling fast! I applied to the Jerusalem and the East Mission, as the advertisement directed. The Bishop was one of my referees and I was appointed in May 1939, my contract being signed for two years.

Then my golden ball fell to the ground and began to unravel and tangle. On 3rd September, a lovely sunny day, war was declared against Germany. Would it be the forces for me after all? Would there be any possibility of getting to Jerusalem? Ought I to go? Memoranda began to drop through the letter-box, post after post. The seventh memorandum brought the news that the Government wanted the overseas schools to remain open; they considered it important for morale and for maintaining loyalty to our side in the war. They would not hold us to our contracts if, in the circumstance, we wished to withdraw. They did, however, hope we would fulfil them. We must be prepared for anything; home leave could not be guaranteed; we could be away for the duration.

I discussed everything with my father and my very dear stepmother. I was an only child, which made it extra difficult to leave them. They, who had experienced World War 1, could see the danger better than I. However, when my father said, "My dear, it is your life; if you want to go, if you think you ought to go, that is what you should do." So I went.

Many weeks elapsed before passages could be arranged for such relatively unimportant people as school staff. I passed my time while waiting by packing essential luggage and by helping to pack babies into those horrible gas masks, for gas was thought the most dreaded weapon the enemy might use.

I had occasional forays into the centre of London. I went and bought our blackout material from Barkers. Another day, I met Guy Fletcher. We who were just down from the universities, were still young, naïve and relatively optimistic and carefree. I remember our walk through St. James's Park. We laughingly wondered why there were so many bird tables, obviously new and recently erected and rather a garish yellow in colour. I afterwards learnt that they were not there for bird preservation, but they were one of those small, rather pathetic attempts to provide for human preservation – they were gas detectors! After that, I never saw Guy again. Soon, he was in the Air Force. I remember the silly comment of a mutual friend – obviously hiding some deeper thoughts – "He has chosen the Air Force because the blue uniform will go best with his blue eyes".[1] He was a young man of considerable promise and soon gained promotion and became an adjutant. Then he was killed – just one of those many young men whose gifts were lost to the world, and an only son. And here am I at eighty-three, writing this.

Eventually, a passage was obtained for me, a third class passage on an Italian ship – 'nothing better available.' The "take what comes" of the war had already begun. I have no note or recollection of my sailing date; I only know that that was the last Italian vessel to sail from our ports before Italy entered the conflict on the other side. It was lucky that we did not have a few more days at sea, as we would then have been sailing on an enemy vessel and, at best, I suppose interned. No enmity on board was directed against us. We were surprised when we heard that Italy had aligned herself with Hitler and I feel sure that at least some of the crew were as surprised as we were. Italy had been a favourite place of the British and we found, on visiting Italy after the war, that we were warmly welcomed back. Italians nostalgically remembered how many of our people had lived and loved in Italy: Romantic poets, Browning and his Elizabeth with her spaniel Flush; Ruskin writing his "Stones of Venice", in the very house where we stayed. We heard often of him and of the elegant, art-loving English spinster ladies who came regularly in the 19th and early 20th centuries.

I travelled with three other members of the Jerusalem Girls' College staff. They had been home on leave and had elected to return. I remember their names: Hester Wood, Elizabeth Noyes and Marjorie Blagden. (They all married in Palestine before the war ended). They were all a few years older than me and Marjorie was the Deputy Head of the school. As time went on, we became good friends, but eventually I lost touch and wish I hadn't.

Marjorie was tall, elegant and aristocratic in manner, daughter of a Bishop, and an Oxford history graduate. She led our little party aboard; a steward immediately relieved us of most of our hand luggage. We ascended to an upper deck. He then asked the numbers of our cabins. His face fell and he nearly dropped our luggage as our Deputy Head, with her natural

---

[1] As it turned out, Guy Fletcher's eyesight was not good enough for the Royal Air Force so instead he enlisted in the Royal Artillery.

dignity, said quietly but clearly, "We are travelling third". Queen Mary could not have done it better. We were then conducted to our shared 4-berth cabin in the bleaker depths, but soon afterwards, we were told that the whole ship was open to us and we could use the first class deck. Whether they were sorry for us being at war, or whether it was just Italian hospitality and dislike of rules, I do not know. There was just a washbasin in our cabin, the floor was bare and may have been concrete. It was very chilly, but as we were going into warmer climes, that might even prove a blessing. The meals were monotonous, lots and lots of pasta. We, Christian Mission staff, were not so pious as to refrain from envious thoughts when some Jewish passengers were given different dishes; we longed for a change.

Eventually, we reached Genoa, where we had a night and a day (or perhaps slightly longer). We even changed for dinner. I remember this because I wore some black shoes, discreetly silver-adorned; I left them under my bed at night, forgot them and, of course, never saw them again. We did a little sightseeing and I remember "our leader" of stately mien doing a little arguing with a taxi man over his charges. I remember nothing of the sightseeing. From Genoa, we sailed to Alexandria; Europe left behind, the Middle East beginning. I resolved, "Egypt, land of the pharaohs; one day I will return." My imagination had been fired when Carson discovered the tomb of the boy Pharaoh Tutankhamen (or Tutankhamun, as he is now known) in 1922.

It was a haunting story, leaving a ghost in my mind that must be exorcised. But not now. We were soon speeding away by train. We travelled by night; I slept well, till Marjorie wakened me to see the sunrise over the desert. It was cold, but before long the temperature was rising. This was my first day in the East.

At last, we reached Palestine. I could scarcely believe it. To be in Palestine was unreal, but how ordinary it was being bundled into a taxi. It was a six-seater; even so I don't know how it took us and all our luggage. In those days, one even carried hatboxes.

A certain apprehension overtook me. What if I couldn't teach after all? I was essentially on my own. I felt dazed, fazed and everything became hazy about me. I was told we had reached Lydda. I opened my eyes and, for the first time in my life saw bougainvillea cascading over a white wall. There was something reassuring about its beauty. My fear for the future was dispelled. "I am going to like this country." Flowers have restorative powers; they scatter joy as they scatter petals.

A Russian Icon of St. George

I was told that St. George was born in Lydda (or Ludd, as it is now called). St George of England, his birthplace in Palestine. I felt welcome. And he was a soldier-saint. "St. George protect our soldiers." Lydda is an airport. Are planes the modern dragons? How many will soon be breathing fire, or be shot down in flames? But Palestine looks peaceful and Jerusalem grows nearer. I remember little more of the journey but a distant vision of ochre-pink hills, and some trees which I was told were apricots or mish-mish. New sights, new names, a new world.

I had forgotten about my golden ball, but I had no need to throw it; it was rolling along fast. We were approaching Jerusalem – The Eternal City – it's origins lost in time. Jerusalem remains forever in my mind as a golden city; a city built of golden stone, radiant in golden light.

Jerusalem, 300 years ago

On first seeing Jerusalem, I was overwhelmed, speechless, amazed that I could be there.

In my mind, I always like to share my experiences with others. How did other earlier travellers arrive in Jerusalem and how did they describe their first sight of the city?

In 1496, one Margery Kempe gave her account of her arrival:

"So they went forth into the Holy Land till they could see Jerusalem. And when this creature (humbly referring to herself) saw Jerusalem, riding on an ass, she thanked God with all her heart then for the joy she had... She was on the point of falling off her ass, for she could not bear the sweetness and grace that God wrought in her soul. Then two pilgrims, Duchemen, went to her and kept her from falling; one of them, a priest, put spices in her mouth to comfort her, thinking she had been sick. And so they helped her on to Jerusalem."

Outside the City Walls

About 400 years later, in 1883, a lady called Esmé Scott-Stevenson wrote:

"After crossing a brook, we wound up a bleak hillside and found our-selves on a breezy undulating plateau ... and in a few minutes more gained our first view of the Holy city.

We were probably there on the very spot where so many way-worn pilgrims and crusaders had in bygone years fallen down and kissed the sacred ground ... We did not emulate them, but the first view of the city is involuntarily accompanied by a flood of thought too full to be expressed, however feebly, by words. No-one can look on Jerusalem unmoved; the first sight of the city must be a solemn moment; there is nothing like it in the world, and one feels then what one probably never feels twice in a lifetime.

It was just sunset; floods of fire and flame were spread over the horizon, above which heavy clouds of deepest purple were closing down, crimsoning the bare, flat hills and distant domes, above which a strange orange glow was hanging in the air. Away to the right stretched the wilderness of Judea, the rounded hilltops, strewn with heaps of grey limestone, stretching as far as the eye could see in the uncertain light and deepening from pale blue into indigo, while further still, on the horizon, were the distant mountains of Moab – "une ligne droite tracée par une moin tremblante" – gradually changing from rose colour to violet, till the glory faded away and the stars came out...

Quoted by Gerald Butt in 'The Lion in the Sand'

Kenneth Cragg, 1939 (Bishop Cragg) arriving in Jerusalem from Haifa in shared taxi, "We crested the hill to the north of Jerusalem. The view is not quite as vivid as that approaching from the east when you come from Bethany over the crest of the Mount of Olives and the whole temple area bursts into view. This could be the place where Jesus wept over Jerusalem, according to the gospel. The northern approach in 1939 was somewhat the same, though not quite so dramatic. I remember the vista of the domes and the towers and the flat roofs and the thrill of seeing them. It's really an entrancing experience, that first sight of Jerusalem. And I remember on that northern hill singling out the two towers of St. George's Cathedral, very English-looking, very Edwardian, rather like Magdalen College tower in Oxford, though of course very recent.

It was not long before the eternal city, the great city of history, retreated from my mind. Our very modern taxi was entering a modern suburb, still built largely of honey-gold stone, but without the patina of age. This was Rehavia. The largest building was the Jewish Agency (later to become the temporary seat of the Jewish parliament). We passed several educational establishments and at last drew up at a comparatively small building; it was but a fragment of the honey-coloured stone, sober and unassuming. It was the Staff House of the Jerusalem Girls' College. Behind it were other buildings within a compound, a stone-spattered compound with a scattering of trees, which I soon learnt were red-berried coral-red pepper trees.

The Staff House – Jerusalem Girls' College

We entered and were welcomed, the others as old friends and I as the new girl. Behind the courtesies for me, there was naturally some analysing scrutiny. I took no instant likes or dislikes and hope they did not either. I knew I was to live for a while in an atmosphere of neutrality, then friendships would come. For a time, staff neutrality was acceptable, but when I met the girls, I knew that I must quickly gain approval – or ever regret my coming. I must quickly reach the point when they wanted to gain my approval. When some people heard that I was going straight from college abroad to teach, they had said: "It won't count towards your pension" and "You ought to have some home experience first." The pension comment I dismissed at once; sixty or sixty-five is too far removed from the early twenties to worry about that. The second comment I think proved untrue. I believe it was easier for me to adapt to the foreign "climate" in every sense than for colleagues who had inevitably developed preconceived school ideas which made them that little bit less adaptable to something different.

Immediately behind the Staff House there was a hard tennis court enclosed with wire screening, gracefully draped with passionflowers. Beyond that rose the Boarding House, an almost handsome building approached by a flight of steps leading to a portico and wide entrance doors. To the side of the building, there was a small verandah. Opposite, to the right, lay the main, lighter coloured, more modern school buildings. Discreetly behind the Boarding House, not immediately visible, there was a long, often-disregarded structure called the Old Hall. Nearby was a gateway for vehicles.

The Boarding House became my home. I had an upstairs room looking towards the staff house.

The Boarding House – Jerusalem Girls' College

HOME for the first few months was often in my thoughts. I was always looking for letters from home and soon I learnt that disruption of postal services was one of the first accidents of war. Letters might take six weeks; if labelled Air Mail, they might travel by sea; they must only be a certain weight; they might be opened by censor; some letters never got through.

Nevertheless, much of what I write in this memoir is largely based on letters I sent home. When I eventually had to close my parents' house in Kent, I found that they had kept the letters I sent them. The bundle cannot have been complete; perhaps some never got through. I would have liked more complete accounts from them, as I never kept a diary. Towards the end of the war, we wrote on airgraphs (see over). Only one page could be used, which was then photographed; no room for long descriptions of what one was doing. Some of the letters have made me wary of the tricks memory can play. For instance, I might remember doing something with two people only to find the name of a third person mentioned in a letter;

so that the truth I tell may often be less than the whole truth. Forgive: there is essential underlying truth, if not accuracy in every detail, as I have claimed in my foreword.

I arrived in Jerusalem sometime in October; the 9th, perhaps. Although somewhat shy and bewildered at first, by 11th November I was writing:

> *"You will be glad to hear that I am now getting quite used to it all here. I think I shall like it very much when I am really at home in all my jobs. I teach only English and only the senior girls. Many of them are very charming and I am extremely fond of them already. One feels all the time what a good school it is ... I have had a grand day today, have enjoyed every lesson I have given..."*

Clearly, my first impressions were very good.

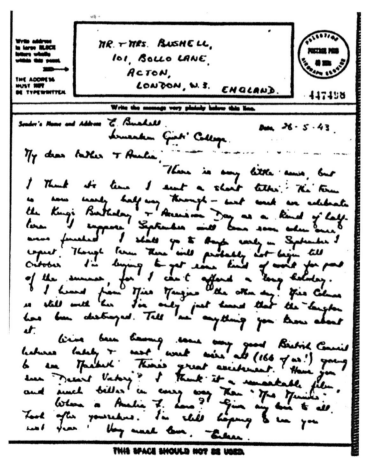

Air graph – actual size!

Note: "The Langton" mentioned in the Airgraph was my old school, the Simon Langton Grammar School, Canterbury. The original form was larger. To save space and weight, the form was photocopied onto microfilm and the film flown out to its destination. On arrival, the message was enlarged and printed out for delivery. I owe this explanation to Captain Fullarton.

I must just tell you that "all my jobs" included synchronising clocks, a job given to the youngest member of staff. At home, I imagine, that was always done by a janitor or caretaker. I didn't like the job much, but I was getting used to it when I stood on a chair to put right the clock just inside the main school door and then, to my horror, I found it looked as if it had been burnt. It was a wooden clock and, looking closely, I found that it certainly had been burnt. I reported the fact and then thought, "Who on earth would do such a thing? They don't really know me; will they think I am a bit barmy?" I began to feel there was something sinister about it. In the end, the H.M. decided it must have been the handyman, who was a little odd. He could carve clever designs on eggshells, which he presented to the housekeeper, but it was agreed that he was simple. I was scarcely aware of his existence. I had been warned that one must be much more profligate with "Good mornings" than at home and had gone out of my way to greet local members of staff and any nearby girls as I went into school in the morning. I might have slighted that handyman, as I seldom saw him. Perhaps I had omitted to say good-morning to him and so he had a grudge against me. That little episode soon passed from my memory but it came back to me a few hours ago!

Here, I should stop and tell you something of the school, its set-up and its purposes. I have a magazine of July, 1939 that was sent to me before going out and I will refer to that and to other sources from time to time.

In 1919 a Girls' High School was started in a German Orphanage building, known as Talitha Kumi (Maiden, arise), formerly run by Kaiserwerth deaconesses. The Relief Fund which supported it was seeking to close its operations; however, the Bishop, Rennie MacInnes and others, wished that the school should continue. The British authorities and Jewish, Moslem and Christian parents all wanted it to do so. A committee was formed under the Bishop. The Church Missionary Society, the London Jews Society, the British Syrian Mission and the United Free Church of Scotland formed a board of management and the school was then, for a time, called the British High School. It is interesting to see that the school was quite "broad-based" ecumenical from its earliest days.

Miss Mabel Warburton, the first Principal, was a lady of vision, "a real pioneer and an outstanding educationalist." She had been in Egypt and then in charge of the British Syrian Mission Training College in Beirut before 1914. I was told that the Government was so anxious to secure her services for the new Jerusalem school that she was quickly brought to Palestine by the Royal Navy. In no time, she had secured a well-trained staff of eight ladies (who took little or no salary, I was told), and very soon the school moved into purpose-built buildings in the suburb of Rehavia and the name was changed to "The Jerusalem Girls' College". "College" was suitable as, for a time, there was a small department for training primary teachers, and also candidates were prepared for the Palestine Diploma, which aimed to give able young people some academic study beyond secondary school level. (Those departments came to an end soon after I arrived). I remember the Headmistress. assigning to me diploma work. I was a little taken aback, but she said that the newly graduated staff had the advanced work fresh in their minds. No argument! The diploma was soon discontinued for lack of staff, or candidates, I believe.

Between 1919 and 1939, the school gained an enviable reputation in Britain as well as in the Middle East. Several times I was told I was lucky to be going there. It seems that it had two or three main aims: many girls came from leading families and, for them and for others, we sought to develop leadership of the highest quality; we sought also to strengthen the Christians who were a minority; we sought, perhaps above all, to bring a reconciling spirit to our work, to bring up a generation where Jews, Arab Christians, Arab Moslems and others who came could all live together in peace.

1919-1939 had not been easy years politically. There had been satisfaction, even rejoicing, when the Turks were replaced by the British as the governing people, but the question of a Jewish homeland and the Balfour declaration led to Arab 'troubles'. Yet I never experienced any 'radical' quarrels in the school. Our aim for tolerance and understanding seemed to be working. The school had no motto, but I think its ideal was 'Love thy Neighbour'. We aimed to be a Christian school in the best sense; we aimed to 'convert'; to turn people from whatever was harmful to others and hence to themselves. Formal conversions to another religion were not permitted by law until a person was at least 21.

When parents came to enter their daughters in the school, they were reminded that we were not just an English-teaching school, but a Christian school. They were told that every girl was expected to attend morning assembly; it symbolised our unity. Everyone could make what mental reservations she felt necessary, but we were all there to learn about each others' beliefs and way of life so that we could show greater tolerance and understanding of one another. For the same reason, there was no withdrawing from Scripture lessons and every member of staff taught Scripture to her own form. Scripture was never 'stinted' as in some schools at home. It had its place with all major subjects on the time-table. Most of us had no particular training for this and I found that preparation took a lot of time. One could not be ill-prepared before our mixed classes. In front of one would sit a group of girls of very varying background; Moslems, who were the most passive, perhaps because Islam teaches them 'acceptance'; Christians of different churches or denominations and various nationalities. Greek Orthodox, Russian Orthodox, Armenian, Coptic, Assyrian, American Protestant, Anglican and German Lutheran, I taught them all in one class. Jewesses, local from long-established families, new refugees from Latvia, Romania, Poland, Germany itself and any other state threatened by the Nazis. I had one girl, a Czech who had been separated from her parents when very young, brought up in an Anglo/French convent and reunited, as a teenager, with her parents in Palestine, only to find that they had no common language!

The Jewesses enlivened the lessons considerably, some knowing the Old Testament better than their teacher! Sometimes their different interpretation of a Scripture passage aroused keen discussion, never disruptive argument. They say you learn more about teaching in practice than in training. I learnt in those lessons how stimulating the honest exchange of knowledge and ideas could be; how good it could be too, to listen and not to lecture. I had many an opportunity for humility resulting from the pleasure of being with minds potentially more able than my own (this was something I particularly appreciated back in England later, when I was teaching sixth formers up to University Scholarship standard). If a teacher has the right relationship, it never does any harm to say "I don't know – but I'll try to find out.") The enthusiasm for learning, especially of the Jewish girls, was most rewarding. I know for certain that with many hindrances, some learnt that inestimable lesson: go on learning anywhere, any time, from anybody, from those less schooled than oneself – and certainly from those you once taught.

I should perhaps state that the school had a majority of Christian Arabs. The ratio when I arrived was roughly 100 Christian Arabs, 70 Muslim Arabs and 40 Jewesses. The total number in the school at any one time was affected by the current political situation. (This was a very sad situation at the end of the mandate. The school dwindled to almost nothing and was eventually closed.)

Most of the staff were English or Scots. The ecumenical nature of staffing had, if anything, increased from the early days, although the management had become more limited. There were also Christian Anglo/Arabs, Arabs (non-Anglican), Armenians and one delightful Jewish lady scholar who taught Hebrew. A younger London University Jewess joined us later and helped me with the teaching of English. Two converts from Judaism also worked with us for a while. Arabic was taught by a master.

Christian schools still exist in Israel. I think our schools were closed because the Israeli Government wanted all Jewish children educated in Jewish, Hebrew-speaking schools. As I have said, we wished to help reconciliation by educating Jews and Arabs together.

Christianity and Islam side-by-side in Jerusalem.

A typical Arab village – once Sheafat, the City of the High Priests.

2. Early Contrasting Outings

Jerusalem Souk, Zebabdeh Village, The Dead Sea

My first outing I recorded in a letter home on 11th November, 1939. It was an obvious one to be the first. Miss Moore, who had been on the staff for many years, kindly took me into the Old City one Saturday. I wrote:

> *"It is the most fascinating place – narrow, crooked streets, many of them covered over, or partly covered over, with roofs and, along each side, stalls of every conceivable kind – Arabs moving to and fro everywhere in their flowing garments – donkeys jostling, old women in dark embroidered dresses squatting at corners, small children threading their way among the crowds – everything colourful, noisy and, to me, exciting. As I often returned to the Souk, I will tell you more about it later".*

Shopping in the Souk.

By the end of January, I was writing about an interesting holiday period and concluded with a description of a visit to a quite different remote village of Samaria called Zebabdeh.

> *"The Bishop was going there to take his annual service and we were invited to join his party. We set off from Jerusalem just after 7 a.m. and had a glorious drive through the hills. The road twists and turns in*

an incredible fashion as it winds upward and then down again into the valley. The places one passes, besides being very beautiful, have names full of associations – the Valley of the Robbers, the Hill of Samuel, with Well of Olive Oil, and so on. First of all, we went to the Mission Hospital in Nablus, and there met the Bishop, Mrs Graham Brown (his wife), Dr Pigeon and Salamo the priest of Nablus. We had tea and biscuits there and then the whole party set out for Zebabdeh, the Bishop's car leading the way. The view was still glorious and we drove for some miles along towards Haifa.

Then we turned onto a side road that looked like nothing more than a cart track. It seemed as if it could not possibly lead anywhere, but when we got a little way along, we found it was being made up and there was a traction engine and donkeys in the path. One of the donkeys was just a tiny thing: it was so sweet (perhaps it was then that I fell in love with donkeys!)

Baby donkey.
My first love!

When we got nearly to the village, all the people were waiting there to meet the Bishop and he walked with them all into the village. The rest of us followed in the cars. It was a great day for the village and we felt rather like a royal procession as we walked between the small stone or mud houses to the slightly superior building which is church and school and house of the Catechist. For a long time, we sat in the tiny sitting room while the chief people of the village and the priests of the Catholic (Latin) and Orthodox (Greek) churches came to pay their respects to the Bishop. We drank much coffee and much tea and the conversation was rapid in English and Arabic and all very pleasant and friendly. There was no fixed time for the service. These people have no clocks and simply wait for the church bell to ring. Finally, it was decided that the service might begin and we went downstairs to the church. All the men sat at the front of the church and the women at the back. Some of the women wore very gay dresses and all the children were very good and gazed at us in a kind of awe and wonder!

After the service, we had a grand feast on the roof, of turkey stuffed with rice and cedar nuts and soup and cauliflowers and Arab bread which one pulls to pieces, never cuts, and fried potatoes. After that, we talked to a few more people and then came back in the Bishop's car to Nablus, where we met members of the Nablus congregation for tea".

This Zebabdeh visit must have taken place at the beginning of January 1940: by 4th February that first year, I was telling of a Sunday trip to the Dead Sea with Marion Gilmour, Hoppy, an Australian Rhodes scholar in the Administration, and a friend of his.

I again described the views as glorious and noted that the road dropped down 4,000 feet. We saw very few signs of life – a few goats, a few sheep and a lone shepherd.

> *"It was wonderfully warm down there and we bathed in the Dead Sea. Of course, you can't sink in the waters. I was very happy just floating on the surface!"*

I am glad I saw the Dead Sea when things were dead down there. The landscape was such that one pondered the fate of Sodom and Gomorrah – perhaps they disappeared below the waters at the time of an earthquake. We tried to identify the pillar of salt that was the wife of Lot, but I believe that also has melted below the waters – although many strange land formations nearby could once have been the naughty lady!

> *Here is no water but only rock*
> *Rock and no water and the sandy road*
> *The road winding above among the mountains*
> *Which are mountains of rock and without water*
> **T.S. Eliot: The Waste Land**

Today, if you visit the Dead Sea, there are hotels and after-bathing showers to wash off the salt. Now you can buy cosmetic preparations prepared from the Dead Sea salts.

Would you like a few facts about the Dead Sea? It is about 1,340 feet below sea level. Over time, it has risen and fallen to a certain extent. Long ago, it was called Lake Jordan and Josephus called it the Asphalt Lake. It was also known in the Bible as the Salt Lake. It is approximately 47 miles long and 10 miles wide. The mean depth is 1,080 feet and its greatest depth 1,310 feet. Its evaporation is extremely high. This is said to account for the peculiar blue-white clouds forming ethereal mists over the surface, adding to the eeriness of the region. The salinity of the Dead Sea is 4-5 times that of ocean water, about 25% saltiness. The Dead Sea contains chlorine, sulphate, sodium, calcium, potassium, magnesium

and bromine. Valuable mining of the last three now takes place.

Note: 1998: There are now fears that the Dead Sea might dry up. With growing populations in Israel, Jordan and Syria, too much water is being drained from the River Jordan, which feeds the Dead Sea, and increasingly higher temperatures are causing greater evaporation.

Early and Easy Shopping

Let us go shopping today, not in the Souk, but in the modern town. We will go down Ben Yehuda Street, where we can get most things we are likely to want and even find a coffee shop for a hot or cold drink or an ice-cream.

The first time I remember buying anything in Jerusalem was when Marion Gilmour came with me, seeking new dresses to supplement the few it had been possible to bring out in hand luggage. The delay in the arrival of my main luggage caused me some anxiety. I wrote in an early letter home at the beginning of November:

> "I heard from Mr Matthew (at the London office of J & EM) the other day. He said that my trunk containing my books and the little one which was left behind are both on their way now. I do hope they come soon. I am not quite sure which presents the greater difficulties: being without books, or half one's clothes! I had to buy another cotton dress, as it was very hot when we first arrived [in October]."

On 4th February, 1940, I wrote that my luggage had just arrived. A letter had taken just over a week then, the luggage 3 months. I continued: "You can imagine how glad I was to see my trunks again. They had been carefully done up in sacking and considering how long things had been packed, everything was in very good condition. It is so nice to have my books and notes".

The cotton dress mentioned I do not remember, but the one I bought when Marion accompanied me I remember well. It became one of those old friends one hates to part with. It was a soft grey silk 'shirt' dress with a prettily half-pleated skirt. Before the war, silk summer dresses were worn frequently. I remember the staff coming to my own school in them when I was still a schoolgirl in the early 1930's – when I wore navy and white cotton!

Later, I found a favourite shop where they made dresses to measure in materials of one's choice. Another shop made up underwear, including all kinds of 'foundation garments'. As the war progressed, re-makes became a speciality. Even hats could be turned back to front and inside out. I am not quite sure about upside down! (I still have an inside-out one!) All this work was done by Jewish refugees, both men and women. I also discovered a treasure of a dressmaker, a Viennese Jewess. I remember two dresses she made for me. One was pale pink with delicate black squiggles on it. The other, a great favourite till long after the war, was mauve shantung with white spots. This I associate with Easter. Rashly, I suppose, I wore it when I went to the Holy Fire service on Easter Saturday. Amidst the great crowd – you might call it a scrum – I was led to a seat on a dais next to a Greek princess. Either I had been mistaken for someone important (I did have a ticket) or my favourite dress made me look like a special guest! However, it was very nice to be comfortable in what has been known to be even a dangerous crowd. I suffered nothing at all. The princess's white dress got a few splashes of candle grease! (See my full account of the Holy Fire elsewhere).

Still on the subject of buying clothes – one of the great joys in Jerusalem was Garabadian's hand-made shoes. They were not then beyond my means, I am very glad to say. Mr G. measured one carefully and then the materials were chosen and the craftsmanship was superb. Whenever anyone said I was like a mountain goat, a gazelle or a fawn, leaping down a hillside, I said "Thank Garabadian". As you can tell from his name, he was an Armenian. Always trust an Armenian artist or craftsman.

Me, in my "battle dress"

One day, I visited the good lady who made my favourite dress to have something altered. She commented on the good material of the suit I was wearing. We got talking and she said "You know, I can re-make anything for you if you will just unpick it completely. It can be cleaned or washed, carefully pressed and then I can re-cut it." I had a heavy shantung suit remade to a more modern style and a blue one that I wore in the Palestinian winter which was made into a battle-dress model, bringing me right up to date. They became great favourites and a blessing, as new materials were becoming very expensive or unobtainable. After the war, this very clever and helpful dressmaker went to America where, someone told me later, she became a couturier of considerable eminence and, as a great favourite with American women, her days of immigrant poverty were well behind her. I was so glad for her; she deserved success.

Except for the necessities of life, I shopped very little. Occasionally, I would buy a book. From time to time, I got as far as looking at rugs or 'Persian' type silver-ware. We always had finger-bowls for our fruit at lunch or dinner and I wanted some to bring home but, whenever I was about to enter a shop for these treasures, a colleague at my elbow would say "Wait till you are going home. Where will you store them?" and "After the war there will be more choice." I wish I had not listened to her good sense for, by the time I came home at the end of '45, we had been 'invaded', not by the enemy, but by our allies, mainly Australians and particularly Americans, whose fatter pockets soon sent the prices up beyond the reach of my modest salary. Also, I left from Haifa, not from Jerusalem, which had the better shops.

Street sign

I did bring home a small collection of Hebron glass. Glowing blue in colour and usually with attractive irregularities, it has been made ever since Roman times. It was the Romans who taught the art. As is usual, my most interesting pieces have been broken, but I have a little left. Similar blue glass is now made elsewhere.

I have often wished that I had bought something from the Ohannesian Potteries. I visited them and saw the quality of their work. I knew the Ohannesian sisters and met their mother and the gifted young men responsible for the artistry and craftsmanship of the tile and pottery, which was excellent. They made tiles for repair work at the Dome of the Rock and also for the elegant, three-language street names that the British installed soon after they took over in Palestine in 1918.

On Friday nights, Jewish shops have to close at sundown. One Friday, I had just completed a purchase and was having a little final chat, when a bearded, fur-hatted old Jew suddenly appeared, loudly blowing his Ram's Horn! The law says it's time to close. I hastily retreated and the shutters were immediately pulled down.

Shofar – Ram's Horn

3. Weather Ways and Weather Wise

When you are travelling in hot countries,
*   the primary rule is to bring your winter clothes*
Gertrude Bell

"Wind upon the wild sky
Like Van Gogh's paintbrush wild with pain"
L Aaronson

There was a roaring in the wind all night
The rain came heavily and fell in floods
But now the sun is rising calm and bright
Wordsworth

The weather of Palestine is delightful – It is also variable, unpredictable, capricious and even devastating.

When I arrived in Jerusalem in October, the weather was hot, summer dress weather. On 6th December, in a letter home, I said "It is still quite warm here in the day time. We wear costumes and woolly things. It has rained a little, just enough to make a few blades of grass spring up."

One year, I remember, it was warm enough for summer dresses and cardigans almost till Christmas day. Another year, Christmas time was as snow-clad as any carol would make us think it ought to be.

At home, our weather is an everlasting topic of conversation; when we can think of nothing else to say, we talk of the weather. On first arriving in Palestine, one rejoices in what seems to be unfailing sunshine. Sunshine is taken for granted, but it is water that is the great concern. I read somewhere that, in an earlier period, the newcomer meeting a local would find that the most interesting thing he had heard about Britain was that it was a land where there was always water. Palestine has always been an agricultural land and it is very important that the rain comes at the right time. Rain is eagerly awaited. I noticed in school the excitement when the first rains came; noise rose several decibels in celebration. The Bible tells us how great is the boast that God "will give the rain for your land in its season, the early rain and the later rain, that you may gather in your grain, and your wine, and your oil. And He will give grass in your fields for your cattle, and you shall eat and be full." For centuries, these were almost all that was asked.

The normal weather pattern for the year leads one to expect that from mid-May to mid-September day after day will be much the same. The sun rises early into a cloudless sky and very soon it is really hot; any variation from this is due to the land situation of a particular place – height (hill-top or valley) nearness to the sea or the desert. The full rainy season is from the beginning of November to the end of March. But there is also a transitional period of uncertainty and expectation – late September and October and again in April and the first half of May. The terms Former and Latter rains probably refer to rain in these periods, although some say they refer to the first heavy rains in the November to March period.

It is a great blessing if rain comes early, because the land can be ploughed early (too hard and dry otherwise) and an earlier harvest assured. These early and late (Former and Latter) rains are also an extra blessing because they are gentle and better penetrating; the main rains beginning in November usually can be very heavy and suddenly dry gullies and river beds can become raging rivers and flood the land. At the same time, winds can be wild and the cold season begins, sometimes severe enough for snow. In St. Matthew 7:27 we read: "The rain fell and the floods came and the winds blew and beat against the house and it fell."

Elsewhere among my reminiscences, you will find other comments on weather. It is amazing how climate can affect our way of life, our personalities and characters – even teaching experience! School life certainly differs with the climate. I have told you that, tucked away behind the Boarding House, there was the Old Hall. This was used for school lunches and for very little else. It was quite suitable except when the heavy rains came. Then a large number of girls and the mistress on duty would be scuttling across the compound under a multitude of umbrellas. I used a sunshade. The surprising thing was that these umbrellas were kept up inside the building, for the roof leaked badly and no-one wanted rain diluted soup or soaked bread, etc. etc. I remember girls kindly holding my sunshade over my head to make it easier for me to eat my lunch. I felt a little like an Eastern Potentate under a ceremonial umbrella, only mine was not jewel-studded!

Speaking of jewels brings back pleasanter memories of the first rain. Everyone looked forward to it. Sometimes it came as a complete surprise. I remember wakening one morning and being thrilled when I walked across to the Staff House for breakfast. Little blades of grass had pierced the pale tawny ground overnight and the raindrops gleamed on them. It soon became like a field of emeralds set in gold as the sun shone on them.

Seeing the rain was exciting, but when snow came the girls' excitement knew no bounds. That wonderful stillness of a first snowy morning was soon broken by the cries of delight of those who had never seen snow before. The Headmistress sensibly accepted the mood and said, "This morning we shall abandon all lessons. Those of you who are young and energetic enough, take your classes out into the snow and teach them how to enjoy it. So those of us who were young enough were soon engaged in a 'staff versus girls' snowball match and competing to make the best snowman. The sun shone and the snow melted all too soon for the girls, who might not see another fall during their schooldays. I myself am glad I saw Jerusalem and Bethlehem under snow. We sang "In the Bleak Midwinter" as never before. We even mimed it. It has always been one of my favourite carols.

More dramatic than my snow experience was that of Sir Ronald Storrs. Heavy snow fell in February shortly after he arrived to govern the country in 1918. He tells his story so well that I will let him do it himself for you. Palestine was invested by the densest snowstorm known for many years (telephones broke down and there was no wireless). Sir Ronald and companions had a journey to make; they were forced to abandon car or wagon and horses and decided to ride on horseback. This is how he tells the story:

> "Next day, we set forth again – one of the most dramatically beautiful journeys imaginable – into Jerusalem. The countryside, solemn and deserted, gleamed under the darkness with its own hidden light, like a Transfiguration of El Greco. Much of the road, especially the last few miles, was so hard to distinguish that, leading the way, my horse stepped over the edge into a snow-drift which closed well over the top of my head, to the startled gaze of my companions, as though I had suddenly and in silence been swallowed into the earth." He adds: "In Jerusalem, I found that the Municipal Council and staff has dealt with the situation by taking to their beds!"

How bitingly cold Jerusalem winters could sometimes be is summed up by this extract from a letter: "This is a bad place for chilblains; some of the children can hardly walk with them. I'm hoping I shan't develop them again." (Not having had them since childhood myself).

I have given you a brief summary of the overall climate of Palestine and shared experiences with you of rain and snow. Now another quotation from my letters will move us on to something quite different. The weather can change quite quickly.

On April 9th, 1943, I wrote:

> "It has only just begun to get warm. We have had the worst winter people can remember, long and cold and snow three times. I have some very nice photographs of us playing in the snow and some taken out on the hills gathering flowers."

Another kind of weather that made the Headmistress send us 'out to play' instead of working was the Khamsin, when teaching or learning could become difficult. We had only to go to the end of the road just beyond the school and we came into open country. In the distance lay the Monastery of the Cross, looking as if it belonged to some fairy tale. Queen Helena was said to have discovered, or planted, the three trees, the wood of which was used to make the cross of Christ. It stood amid rocky ground, which could become bejewelled with flowers in the springtime. We jumped from rock to rock and, in the crevices, found myriads of little cyclamen and, here and there, red anemones. In those days the flowers were not protected and we experienced the joy of gathering bunches to take home. I was reminded of my own childhood pleasure in the woods near Canterbury of seeing bluebell carpets and gathering primroses, violets and wild flowers.

The Author and husband on a later visit to the Monastery of the Cross.

That Khamsin was not a bad one, but by May it was much hotter. The weather contrasts became more apparent from a letter I wrote on May 23rd, 1941:

"Yesterday, I took my form and a few other boarders, for a picnic. Form picnics are always a great event, as normally they take place only once a year. We went by bus to Abu Ghosh, about eight miles and half-an-hour's run from here on the way to Jaffa. The road is very hilly and has seven hairpin bends; they call it The Seven Sisters! It was a terribly hot day and many of the cars on the road were having difficulty; all the buses by 3.30 in the afternoon, when we wanted to come home, were going very slowly so that we had to wait 50 minutes in broiling Sirocco (Khamsin). The first bus that came was full; the second took us, but we had not gone far when it stopped; from then it chug-chugged along a few yards, stopped and went, and so on

all the way. When we at last got to town, we (the boarders in the party) all piled into a taxi – and then I bought them ices and so home quite happily."

(Retrospectively, I remember advice not to eat ice-creams or drink iced drinks when very hot!)

"The temperature has been 104-105 degrees in the shade some days lately. I have felt the heat much more this year, but soon May will be out and we shall not have so many east winds and so it will be better."

Wind is probably the worst part of Palestine's climate. There is a devastating wind that blows from the east or south, and most frequently in the transition times of Autumn and Spring, when it often destroys crops. This is the *Khamsin* or *Sirocco*. It is so harsh and dry and hot that to humans it is soul destroying; it can alter personalities. Tempers rise, even to murder point. It is said by some Arabs that murderers should be given mercy if they committed their crimes under the influence of the *Khamsin*. Sometimes, a compensatory blessing comes after the wind changes to the west. At first, one hears the lashing of trees and the clanging of doors and then the descent of rain, the first rain for weeks perhaps, welcome at first, if it does not become a deluge. The long-wished-for rainy period can become a time of drought or drowning.

Yes, Palestine's climate can be capricious.

Kathleen Hatton wrote a poem "East of Jordan" in June 1942, in which she tells how the *Khamsin* could make one homesick for the more moderate moods of our home climate.

Thermometer at ninety-four
The colours bleached from sky and hill
A restless, fretful desert wind
Which frays the nerves and tires the will
Country beloved in other moods
Today be far from me, give place
To that chill land whose friendly rain
Drops as a veil across her face...
   Kathleen Hatton

Capricious is the climate of Palestine; but the washing I put out to dry in Scotland in the sunshine now at the end of the day hangs soaked and sagging in the changeable weather of June. We all have our moods. Remember Palestine's climate is Mediterranean and resembles California – if you know that better.

I still look back and think Palestine's weather was delightful – so much sun. There are times, of course, when distance lends enchantment. Certainly, it was always easy to get up early on a Jerusalem morning and, towards evening, a cool refreshing breeze made one believe in and appreciate the cool of the day – especially in Jerusalem.

Old City, Jerusalem.

A typical village scene in 1940s Palestine.

A Note on Abu Ghosh – Biblical (Kiriath-Jearim) Emmaeus

This area is associated, not only with Cleopas and his friend being joined by Jesus whom they did not recognise until he broke bread and blessed it, but it also commemorates where David rested the Ark. Richard Coeur-de-Lion got no farther than here when advancing on Jerusalem. The Roman 10th Legion was stationed here and there is a stone with an inscription on it to prove their presence. So Romans marched where the tarmac road runs. Crusaders came and built a church; much later victorious Turks, British and Israelis passed the same way.

Impression of Crusader Church and Abu Ghosh Gardens

The church is beautiful and Benedictine monks welcome visitors with crystal clear water from a spring on the site. One can refresh one's spirit with their uplifting plain-song, or simply looking on their plants in pots; they are good gardeners. Watching over the area from a great height is the Madonna of the Ark.

The scenery round about is beautiful. The Rev. Leslie Farmer, who saw it about the same time as I did, said, "Never had I realised the unutterable loveliness of the Holy Land until I sat and saw the view." And when he climbed a minaret at nearby Nebi Samwil, he says, "It commands a better panorama, perhaps, than any building in the land."

On the pathways that Jesus might have trod, you can walk from Jerusalem. (Other sites claim to have been Emmaeus, however.)

The name Abu Ghosh is interesting. It came from a man named Abu Ghosh, who was a bit of a rascal, a charming one, it seems; a chieftain, a brigand, a sheik, a bandit and, undoubtedly, a person of consequence. I think he also knew how to get on with the right people. He normally exacted taxes on anyone passing through his district to Jerusalem but he met

Lady Hester Stanhope with courtesy and hospitality, killing a sheep for her dinner cooked by his four wives. Then, at night, as a mark of honour, he himself kept guard over her encampment.

Emmaeus

The Anglican Bishop, Gobat, tried to convert and reform Abu Ghosh, without success. Later, the 'old scoundrel' returned to reclaim acquaintance with His Grace, bringing him the gift of a silver vase, the history of which has never been revealed!

4. War and Peace

Pray for the Peace of Jerusalem
Pray not for Arab or Jew
for Palestinian or Israeli
But pray rather for yourself
That you may not divide them in your prayers
But keep them both together in your hearts

I do not want to talk war. I do not want to talk politics, but like the weather, they influence life.

As I write in 1998, we know that the Jews and Arabs, although not officially at war, are attacking one another politically and from time to time dreadful massacres are perpetrated. For several years before I went to Palestine, the situation had been very similar, except that the British were then the government under the mandate set up after World War 1. They were trying to keep peace between Jew and Arab. The Jews were seeking a homeland and the Arabs were afraid of losing one. At that time, the Arabs were attacking the government and from time to time, placing bombs (often home-made) in order to bring the British round to their side. But when war was declared against Germany, both Jews and Arabs decided to bury their grievances and support Britain as being the better bet for the future than the Nazis would be.

When I arrived in Palestine, the 'troubles' had almost ceased and it all seemed so peaceful that I was surprised when the H.M. was giving me a lift in her small car one day, I saw her on her knees peering under the car. I offered to assist and there were the two of us looking as if we were about to repair the car or saying our prayers in the road, when really we were making sure that no-one had been patriotically placing a small hand-made explosive device to welcome us!

These searches soon ceased and it was not till after VE day that wariness was, alas, called for again. By then, the bomb-makers were the Jews, for the government was severely limiting Jewish immigration, and had turned back desperate shiploads of refugees, diverting them to Cyprus, usually. Many lives were lost through this policy. Trying to be fair to both sides was really an impossible task.

The King David Hotel, where leading members of the government worked, was bombed. My friend, Marion Gilmour was buried under rubble and escaped with her life but mourned her friends who had died, and never forgave the Jews. One of my Jewish girls who hated all that was happening said 'they' were using young boys 12-13, to place bombs. The King David Hotel bomb had been delivered in a milk bottle, with the early morning delivery by an Arab employee who had no idea what deadliness he was carrying.

Our peaceful years between 1940 and 1945 were, of course lived against a background of war. We had anxieties for people at home. Our letters, which usually took many weeks to reach their destination always had paragraphs on the progress of the war. From time to time, we thought the fighting was coming nearer. On August 8th 1940, I wrote: "We have just heard that we are going to have an air raid siren on the roof of the Boarding House, so I'm afraid there will be no sleeping through for us, even in holiday time."

My parents, living on the outskirts of London, were driven at one stage to going up each night to one of the shelters created in Underground stations, but they found that so unendurable that they decided to remain in their own beds and endure the noise of air raids and the awful dropping of bombs around them. They had already moved from Canterbury to London and thus escaped certain death, for their Canterbury home was already destroyed. In London, they escaped with only shattered windows and a mean-minded burglar, who then got in and stole some cherished possessions. The meanness was unexpected and very distressing, as good neighbourliness and trust were generally characteristic of wartime Britain.

Our air raid siren gave us very little trouble. We were all concerned for people at home, but we also had anxieties, at certain times, for ourselves. We did not take our peace for granted. On 16th August, 1941, "There has been a greater sense of security here lately, since the Syrian campaign ended and the Russian war began, but the news from Russia does not seem very good just now ... I wonder when it will all end?" I continued: "My Literary Club is going very well and next week we are going for a picnic ... They wanted what they called a week's picnic, but I could not undertake that with even a faint possibility of air raids; but one might as well let them enjoy themselves as much as possible, while they can".

On April 22nd, 1942, I wrote, with added seriousness: "We have just heard the news about Greece, and the removal of their Parliament to Crete. It is bad, but the war is young yet. No doubt Hitler will hang himself in time. If the war comes here, and I get interned, or anything, don't worry. I'm not afraid. I fear more for our Jewish children than for anything: there are so many of them I am very fond of. I shall try to avoid evacuation if I can. I feel I belong here and if things get bad, I want to stay." This, I know, was genuine fearlessness. Now, in old age, fear comes much more readily.

It must have been about this time that we were told in a government directive that we must pack a small bag with essentials and keep it always handy. Rommel seemed to be doing well and was known to have designs on a Palestine conquest. If, at this point, anyone felt she wished to get home for some good reason, she could apply for the chance of a passage, otherwise it was 'take what comes'. Nothing came, of course; the tide in North Africa began to turn in our favour – and after a few months one of our North African fighting men, following a spell in a desert hospital, was transferred to Intelligence in Jerusalem. He was to become my husband.

You remember our air raid alarm. Well, we had one orderly experience of getting the boarders into our basement shelter soon after they had gone to bed. To soothe their nerves, which did not seem to need soothing at all, we handed round cups of cocoa to them all and they went back to bed laughing and happy. I think there was another disturbed occasion when, the next morning, we were told that the alarm had gone off because a mouse had got into the works. Where had our Bissy gone, to let a mouse penetrate to such a hiding place? ('Bissy' is Arabic for 'pussy' – a word brought home by the Crusaders). Language frequently changes 'B' to 'P'.

I remember one other air-raid experience, recorded in a 1942 letter:

"We had a very nice end of term. We broke up on the Friday and on the Wednesday before we held a Garden Fete to which about 600 people came. Just after the opening, there had to be an air-raid alarm but no-one seemed much depressed by it. Perhaps I fared worst, for the H.M. told me to get the girls into the shelter. Of course, it was impossible to drag them from their parents and friends and, as fast as I got any in at one door, they were through the shelter, which has a dark twisting passage, and out and up the steps at the other end. It was a great game! But that was soon over and side shows and stalls began to do good trade, so that we made £57. (Not a bad sum, since a year's salary was then, if I remember rightly, £180)."

When VE Day came, we shared in the rejoicing. Spontaneously, some of the girls formed themselves into the V sign and had their photograph taken. In the city, there were parades, fly-pasts, flood-lighting, concerts and parties. The expatriates had, at the back of their minds, expectations at last of home-leave and before long the more important people, including Headmistresses, were being flown home. (Flying was still then a novelty and an expensive one.)

The people of the country postponed their thinking of what the future might hold. They saw the marches before the King David Hotel and the handsome YMCA building, little knowing that, in the renewed peace, the 'King David' would soon be shattered, the Mandate ended. Their peace would be uneasy for a long time to come.

For the moment, *together* we all rejoiced.

The girls in 'V' for Victory formation (their own idea).

The End of War Celebrations – The skies lit up – all rejoiced together.

5. Teaching

"Gladly learn and gladly teach"
   Chaucer

"And very sweet it is, while the sunlight waves
In the ripening morning, to sit alone with the class
And feel the stream of awakening ripple and pass
From me to (them)"
   W.H. Auden

I wonder what your own schooldays were like? Whatever they were, don't turn aside from the word 'teaching'. I am not going to expound teaching techniques. Once, when I was in Palestine, I was asked by a Director of Education to discuss my teaching methods. In my youth, and to his horror, I think, I said, "I just teach." Auden expresses it well: what one wants is to "feel the stream of awakening ripple and pass from me to them". Teaching is very personal, very human. As in so much in life, the 'right relationship' is important, but should be almost unconscious. English Literature is a wonderful subject to teach; it, in itself, is profoundly human. It is that profundity which one seeks to pass on, to awaken, as Wordsworth said:

   A sense sublime
   Of something far more deeply interfused
   Whose swelling is the light of setting suns
   And the round ocean and the living air
   And the blue sky, and in the mind of man

There should be an electric current passing from teacher to student and back again – giving and giving back. The 'electric shock' treatment is most necessary. Expose people to poetry. Let the poem speak for itself. Convey your own appreciation quietly; never over-work that, or the poem, just hope for the awakening.

The greatest delight in teaching can be awakening a mind with more potential than one's own. A light "that never was on sea or land" suddenly flashes back. The class is electrified. One of my main aims in writing this 'chapter' and indeed my whole account of time recollected in Palestine, is to show how different teaching abroad can be from teaching at home.

I was lucky to be able to 'teach poetry' in a poetic setting while in Jerusa-Jerusalem. One class I particularly remember: I had four delightful senior girls to teach – one Jewish, one Armenian, one Greek and one Franco American, sitting on the little portico outside the Boarding House on sunny days but sheltered from the direct sun, and looking out towards the passion flowers half-hiding the tennis courts; and in front of them a beautifully shaped almond tree, which added to its own natural beauty a recollection of the trees of Van Gogh's paintings. One watched its unfolding until one said, with Cecil Day Lewis, "Today the almond tree turns pink."

I had another valuable teaching experience in Jerusalem which I have never had elsewhere; I might call it voluntary, although it could not have happened without school approval. From time to time, I took small groups of girls to Ain Karim for Reading Parties. These were not parties in the jolly sense, although they were very enjoyable. It was possible, about 1941-1943, to go to a very comfortable house in Ain Karim for a few days and read and discuss books beyond the syllabus, often suggested by the girls themselves. "MacBeth" was requested because one class had talked about it and another did not want to miss it. Reading was often done out of doors. Spare time walks exploring the countryside were also enjoyed; housework and cooking were kept to a minimum and shared by everyone. The day ended with quiet reading. There were religious and other books on the bookshelves for anyone who wanted them. Cups of cocoa sometimes followed, when settled under the super-soft eiderdowns that the house provided.

An extension of this idea came from some of the girls themselves. One day, when I was on playground duty, I was asked if they could have a Holiday Literary Club during the long vacation, which lasted from July to October, about three months. Such enthusiasm deserved agreement, and so we met either at school or at one of their homes, quite informally and often out of doors. Everyone was invited to make suggestions for the programme; everyone read something at home and then a leader led a discussion. This gave an opportunity to improve fluency and accuracy in spoken English where needed, as well as increasing knowledge in a most enjoyable way – often with parents co-operating and providing delicious refreshments. One certainly had a much greater entry into the girls' homes than is usual in Britain and there it worked to everyone's gain. It was certainly a characteristic of our schools.

I think I told you earlier that I had never felt well equipped for primary teaching. Not having had younger brothers or sisters of my own, I had never wanted to teach small children. It was therefore more of a shock than a surprise when, one day in my first year, I was asked if I would fill a gap in the Junior School and take a lesson for an absent member of their staff. The request came at a moment's notice. Whatever would I teach them? I was wearing a pink shantung blouse, subtly patterned with the story of Cinderella. There was the answer. I walked in, smiled my good-morning, said how nice it was to see them, then invited them to cluster round me and they took it in turns to tell me the story on my blouse, continuing from one another and, of course, learning to speak in perfect English! They ended up asking for another story, another time, – but I had no more obligingly decorated blouses! I was quite converted to teaching little ones! – but no other emergency arose and I was never called back to their class again. I did, however, when crossing the compound, sometimes hear the patter of little feet behind me and then see little smiling faces looking up at me, and perhaps a little hand taking mine. They were my new friends.

The 'Cinderella' Class

Before I continue in a serious vein, I want to give you a quotation from D H Lawrence's poem on "Work":

> *There is no point in work*
> *Unless it absorbs you*
> *Like an absorbing game*
> *If it doesn't absorb you*
> *If it's never any fun*
> *Don't do it."*

I said when I began writing that I would put on my rose-coloured spectacles, but you probably will not believe me if I paint a *completely* rosy picture. I will now tell you of my nastiest surprise. It could only happen in a boarding school and would be most unlikely to happen in Britain. I will lead up to it gently.

Like most young girls contemplating a career, I had for a while thought that I would like to nurse (nursing, teaching, or secretarial work were about all the careers open to us then). I suppose the glamour of the uniform and fancying myself as a ministering angel, attracted me. A spell of scarlet fever, a thumb slashed in a botany class, perhaps introduced the reality of blood and bed-pans to my mind; I decided to teach. I enjoyed gaining knowledge and anything that I discovered that pleased me I found hard to keep to myself; I wanted to pass it on and discuss it with others.

Teaching, however, turned me back to 'nursing' in Jerusalem in a very surprising and disappointing way. On June 29th, 1942 (the same date as I am writing now, by chance, 56 years later), I wrote home:

> "We've been coping with a great deal of sickness. Six girls have now been transferred to hospital; they are all typhoid cases. I got the last one out of the house and into hospital on Friday and this morning I have just finished seeing her mother about her things. We have closed school owing to the epidemic. This was decided on Monday and all the boarders except two had gone by Friday night. The two who were left were sisters and I quite enjoyed having them to myself. It's easier to look after two than fifty! Fortunately, we had got exams over, but Speech Day and the School Play had to be abandoned – so it is rather a flat feeling about the place."

I had no doubts that I preferred teaching to nursing.

Nothing can be more human than nursing, but the relationships formed in teaching are of much longer duration and the memories one has of one's contacts are likely to be more varied. I cannot possibly tell you all that I remember about my J.G.C. girls. Sometimes I remember them by name, but sometimes, although I see them clearly in my mind, their names will not come back to me; not surprising, as now I cannot remember the name of someone I met only a few days ago!

Here are some 'thumb sketches' of a few girls I remember well, perhaps because each had a dramatic or significant story. They were all boarders.

Najah Azzouni was a Christian Arab, her father a successful business man. She was slightly plump, always merry and good-humoured, entirely lovable, of average ability, kind and generous. She made a close friendship with **Rena Aboutaboul**, a Jewish girl, nice but naughty! (This was a closer friendship than usual between Jew and Arab; usually the closer friendships were between 'two of a kind'). Najah failed her School Certificate; we, and she, had though she would make it. When the results came, I found her in floods of tears and crying repeatedly, "I shall never get a husband now!", a contrast there between British and Arab schoolgirls! Certainly, in those days husband problems would not have been the first thought if one failed one's exams; more likely one would have thought of marriage merely as the only option left open! Najah's concern showed a change in this society; men were seeking better educated and more completely companionable wives.

Merije Feldhuns (who liked to be called Mary) was a Latvian Jewess. Her father was already in America seeking to re-establish himself in business there; her mother soon joined him, leaving Mary to the guardianship of her eldest sister's husband. Her two sisters had been educated at Cheltenham Ladies' College; on arrival in Palestine, Mary was sent to a Hebrew speaking co-ed school in Tel Aviv and did not like it. I do not think her sisters had liked Cheltenham either – black woollen stockings and silence rules had not appealed to them. Mary decided that she wanted to come to an English school: the climate would excuse her from black woollen stockings and she could always break a few silence rules. She was not averse to breaking rules! Mary was a girl of character and charm, neat in figure and with a winning smile. She tackled the English language with determination and, with a little extra help, could soon follow all the lessons, and very soon was chatting away in English as easily as in French or German. She could also speak Lettish, which no-one else understood. Her French she had learnt from a short period in a French convent school; her German she had acquired easily from her parents and from her German governess, for whom she had a deep affection.

I learnt Mary's background story one day when she was sitting alone in the playground reading an English book; her first attempt to do that, she told me when I went up and spoke to her. As we talked, I noticed that she was wearing a locket. Jewellery was against the rules, I reminded her gently. She said "Please let me wear this. My governess gave it to me when she had to go back to Germany because of Hitler." She almost hissed the last words. "I told her I would always wear it and remember her. I never hear from her. I do not suppose I will ever see her again." As tears came into her eyes, I said, "Just tuck it in then, so that no-one can see it." We smiled at each other and I left her to her book. Mary married at an early age in America.

Elisabeth and Hildegard (Schmidt) – true surname beyond recall. Elisabeth and Hildegard were daughters of a German Lutheran pastor. He could not bring himself to accept the Nazi code and so, before it was too late, he managed to escape with his wife and two daughters. They arrived in Jerusalem, where they may have hoped to find friends and refuge in the Lutheran Church of the Redeemer and a friendly German presence, but war brought the closure of that church and internment to all Germans, including Pastor (Schmidt). His family also had to endure restricted freedom. His wife was allowed to live in a cottage in a country area, but had to report to the Police regularly; his daughters had to become boarders in the safe care of the Jerusalem Girls' College. I never heard any of the family complain.

Elisabeth and Hildegard arrived wearing their charming Bavarian dirndl dresses. They had long, flaxen pigtails and curtseyed when they were introduced to me. Their manners were impeccable: every morning they repeated their curtsies until I suggested that they might like to adopt the less formal 'good-mornings' customary in the Boarding House.

Their mother, a typical German 'Frau', eked out her very small income by making delicious peanut butter, the first I ever tasted. One year, she invited me to stay with them for their Christmas celebrations, which took place mainly on Christmas Eve. They had a tastefully decorated tree, all white and silver stars and home-made (I saw a similar tree later, when I visited the Jerusalem Leper Hospital run by Moravian sisters under the direction of the devoted and indomitable Sister Johanna). Our Christmas 'feast' was a spaghetti and tomato dish and a simple cake. I thought of the proverb "Better a dish of herbs with love than a roasted ox...." ....or a roasted turkey!

There was another part to my new experience – sleeping under a feather downie for the first time. I had slept on top of a 'feather bed' at my grandmother's when I was a child, but I had never had more than an eiderdown on top of me. The downie was hung out of the window to air on Christmas morning, as I had seen them on a visit to Germany about 1935. After a simple breakfast, we walked in the countryside and rejoiced on finding some early blooming flowers. Quite soon, I left to attend a service at St. George's Cathedral.

I don't think it was on Christmas Day, but on one occasion Elisabeth came with some other girls to a communion service. Someone on the staff then asked if she should have been taken, as she was Lutheran, not Anglican. I simply said, "I think the good Lord will be glad she came. He will understand her situation better than we do."

Sadly, my friendship with Elisabeth cooled because, after she left school, when she heard I was travelling to the Lebanon, she asked me to take a letter across the border for her, thus dodging the rather slow, and possibly censored, postal service. I was strongly advised not to take the letter; it would be illegal and, being from a German, might cause trouble for her, for me and for her intended recipient. It was addressed to a young man, an

American who, I believe, she eventually married. Not unnaturally, she had not informed me about any of its contents. For me, it was just a regrettable incident.

Olga Podborachinska-Rommel (The Rommel was sometimes omitted, not just for length, but because, at that time, 'Rommel' was not exactly a popular name, as his troops were threatening our doorstep). Olga was a beautiful girl, the daughter of a Polish General who had been taken prisoner by the Nazis. Olga and her mother had come to Palestine, leaving behind almost all they owned. Her mother was fighting severe ill-health, T.B. I ws told.

Olga, like so many, adapted herself to life in our boarding house, but gave us one dramatic morning. About 5.30 a.m., I was just thinking it was time I got up, when the Matron burst into my room saying, "You must come at once, quickly now. Olga has cut her wrist." (The thought went through my mind "Not intentionally, surely." I flung on my dressing gown and followed. I could see at once that we must get Olga to hospital without delay. I rang immediately for a taxi and the Matron went with her, while I saw to the clearing up. To my surprise and consternation, I discovered that she had been opening a bottle of Advocaat and had cut her wrist on broken glass. What would the staff of the Mission Hospital think of one of our girls having an alcoholic drink in her locker? (At this distance in time, the thought raises a smile, but it did not at that moment). It turned out that Olga's mother had given the Advocaat to her as a tonic. Tonics were the thing in those days and Mrs P-R, ill herself, was frantically anxious to keep her daughter fit and well.

Later, Olga gave me another shock, to my great sorrow. After leaving school, she became a receptionist at the Jerusalem Officers' Club. I returned to the UK in 1945. One day, I was looking at the *Illustrated London News* in the hairdresser's when, to my horror, I saw pictures of a distraught woman among piles of rubble. It was Olga's mother. The club had been bombed in the renewed Arab/Jewish 'troubles' and the beautiful Olga was dead. Her poor, poor mother.

> *"And of my weeping, something must be left,*
> *which must die now. I mean the truth untold,*
> *The pity of war, the pity war distilled."*
> **Wilfrid Owen**

To conclude on a happier note, shown in the photograph overleaf are two friends, Hildegard (German) and Marija, a Jewess from Poland whose family had fled the German invasion.

Hildegard and Marija at Ain Karim.

Church of the Visitation at Ain Karim.

6.   Redoubtable Ladies

A story was being circulated at one time of a redoubtable lady who had retired home to England after many years of service in the Middle East. She had really left her heart in Palestine and when war broke out she thought it was her chance and her duty to offer her services to the land she loved most, but at her age, something well beyond the usual point of retirement, nobody would support her return and try to arrange her passage. She was a woman of indomitable determination, authoritative and courageous, and eventually she heard of a ship about to set sail on which there had been some cancellations. She therefore proceeded to the port and somehow managed to get on board as a visitor seeing off some legitimate passenger. At some point after sailing time, she stalked along to the Purser's office and demanded a passage to Palestine. What kind of cabin she did not mind, and she showed him enough money to pay for whatever was available. The Purser did not want to oblige her and she then turned to Higher Authority. She dropped down on her knees and invoked the help of the Almighty. The Purser was totally nonplussed. This was a situation he had never met before. The occasion proved to be one of the swiftest answers to prayer ever recorded. The Purser gave in. The lady got back to Palestine, but not to the warmest of welcomes, for something she had not realised, and which many of us find it hard to realise, is that, although we may have taken responsibility in the past, we can become a responsibility to others eventually.

This story may by apocryphal, but it is certainly symbolic of the devotion and indomitable spirit of many Redoubtable Ladies (elderly ladies they seemed to us when young), who served the country nobly in Mandate Days. I have a little book prepared for the forces which has at its end a list of places in Palestine and the church people serving them. Many times, 'Resident Lady Missionary' or a similar term refers to these Redoubtable Ladies. They were scattered all over Palestine. Many of them originally had lost 'sweethearts' in the First World War.

The Redoubtable Lady I came to know best was Miss Joseph. I heard it said that her family had been converted from Judaism to Christianity sometime in the past. She herself dated herself when she told us that as a little girl she had sat on Tennyson's knee and either gave him a red rose for his buttonhole or had taken a red rose out of his buttonhole. It was hard to think of Miss Joseph as a 'dear little girl', for she had obviously become a character whom no-one would trifle with. I soon respected Miss Joseph, liked her and was honoured by an invitation to visit her along with another member of staff. This is how I described the experience in a letter dated 22nd April, 1941:

"Yesterday, I came home from El Husn, an Arab village in Transjordan (near Irbid) where I had been staying for a few days over the Eastern Easter. It was a most interesting visit, quite different from anything I had done before. We stayed with Miss Joseph, the one English person living there. In the mornings, we went with her to her clinic and watched her do eye and ear treatments. Then we paid about a hundred visits to the houses of Greek Orthodox Christians. Some of the dwellings were very primitive, built mostly of mud with no windows, and a tiny yard. Sometimes a house had several rooms, sometimes only one. The men sat drinking coffee and smoking in the best rooms. The women cooked and nursed their babies elsewhere.

Dogs and cats and chickens and goats and sheep and donkeys and camels and sometimes children occupied the yards. Sometimes, the chickens and goats wandered into the rooms where we drank coffee; nobody minded. Some of the rooms were clean, some were squalid; all had rugs on the floor and mattresses ranged round the walls. Usually, we sat on three mattresses but in a few more modern households, we were given chairs.

Impression of the interior of some houses visited

Everywhere, we were received with elaborate courtesy and greetings. The Arabs have nothing to learn from us in natural graciousness, or formal politeness.

At each house, we drank coffee, a few mouthfuls, black and sugarless, from little handle-less cups, rather like egg cups. (Everyone drank from the same cup, so that last night when I felt rather queer, I won-

dered whether I might have typhoid or some unknown disease!) Then we had to take at least one sweet, usually a Needler's Milord Toffee out of a yellow box! – two sweets is correct, but we were allowed to accept only one 'because of the war', they half-jokingly smiled. Even these remote places have radios and know the war news, not always accurately, but in some form or another." They were already becoming aware of economies and shortages.

El Husn, an Arab village in Transjordan

There was more to tell about our visit than that. Before we went we asked what we could take Miss Joseph. We were told: "Take her fresh butter. She cannot get real butter there." So we went to Spinney's, the almost famous Jerusalem grocery store, and somehow we packed the butter so that it would not melt. (I seem to remember some wet newspaper; perhaps we started with ice). When we got to El Husn, Miss Joseph was delighted at the thought of fresh butter; so were we, for we had been warned that our hostess's housekeeping could be a little out of date. She fetched a large flask, opened it and took out – some butter, which proved to be a good deal less fresh than that which we had brought. 'Our' butter we saw popped back into the hastily rinsed flask till the next visitors came. We did not strain Miss Joseph's limited food resources too much, for kind people invited us out. I remember sitting on the floor and delving into a large dish of lamb cooked in leban. It was not unpalatable, but I could not fully appreciate it because I had heard how the honoured guest was often expected to eat an eye. I must avoid that at all costs, I thought, and resorted to hinting in one way or another that my accompanying friend was my superior if not my senior.

The highlight of our visit was to be paying our respects to a Latin Bishop who was making his Easter Visitation. Miss Joseph insisted that we must meet at a certain border point, which turned out to be at Gerash. I wanted to see Gerash and so set off with high hopes. We had to be properly dressed to meet the Bishop (such were ecumenical standards we found, that we must be a good deal more correct than for our own Bishop). We must wear hats and we were presented with a pair of white gloves each to wear for the formal handshake. We also had sunshades. I think we went a certain distance by taxi, in order not to be dishevelled, and then we were dumped on the roadside at a border point and Miss Joseph said we could sit on some nearby boulders until the great man arrived.

"Is this Gerash?" I asked.

Miss Joseph raised her gloved hand in an elegant gesture and said, "The ruins are over there." They were so distant as to be scarcely discernible.

I was not to see Gerash. From time to time, Miss Joseph walked up and down, prodding the earth with her parasol and cloaking her suppressed impatience with an excellent impersonation of Queen Mary. If we moved from our uncomfortable perches, we were soon told to sit down and wait quietly. It was so hot that I thought it was a good thing we didn't wear make-up or it would surely have melted. Thank goodness for the sunshades. At last, the great man's car drew up. There, in this parched, desolate and deserted spot in an outpost of the Empire, we were politely presented to the Monsignor, who managed a brief smile and a few words with Miss Joseph and then went on his way. It was all over.

Still wearing our white gloves, which we had not been allowed to remove, we returned the way we had come. I had been to Gerash – but the chance of a lifetime had been missed. I had seen scarcely anything. It is one of the wonders of the world which I have in my memory as only a near miss, a glimpse of a few broken pillars shrouded in blossom.

Still, I am so glad Miss Joseph invited me.

What I should have seen in Gerash

7. Amman

At the end of December 1941, I went to Amman. I was invited by the Headmistress, Helen Wilkinson, of the Girls' School there, to stay with her for a few days. I wrote in a letter dated 4th January 1942: "Amman is the capital of Transjordan."

Jordan became a kingdom in 1946. It is literally across the Jordan from Palestine and a famous bridge over the River Jordan, known then as the Allenby Bridge, divides them. The bridge is now called the King Hussein Bridge. I wrote then:

> "It is completely Arab and almost completely Moslem. So it gives a very different impression from most of the cities of Palestine. As it was the time of a Moslem feast while we were there, we paid several visits. First of all, we went to the Palace to call upon the Emira. It was interesting to go, but all very simple. After we had made our little curtsies, we just sat around for a while, were given sweets, and then came away."

I expect I was a little disappointed. I may have expected something resembling Buckingham Palace. The Emira was a nice little lady but not at all glamorous, dressed rather drably in brown and fawns and her heavy stockings wrinkled. She spoke very little English; fortunately my friend could talk in Arabic – but conversation was very limited. She received visitors such as us because she was the first wife. There was a second wife, of whom people knew little and whom very few people saw. A new third wife had recently been taken, but she was determinedly kept from prying eyes. She was referred to as the Black Emira; some said she was Sudanese.

Another visit took us to the Boys' School, where the Headmaster and his wife warmly welcomed us. Occasionally afterwards, I met masters from the school who came up to Jerusalem from time to time.

Other visits in Amman? My letter continued; "The next two days we visited the homes of three of our boarders. Our own girls did not talk very much but served us with coffee and sweets; but two of them had sisters who were old girls and they chattered away very happily."

One of our visits was sad. We visited a very nice quiet Moslem girl, who was the only one of our boarders whose parents insisted that she wore a veil and not a school hat. She took us to see her aunt, who had recently been divorced. Moslem divorces seemed to be rare (after all, four wives were permitted) and I heard it said that arranged marriages produced fewer divorces and less unhappiness than the favoured 'love matches' of the west. The divorcee seemed a nice, quiet person like her niece (but rather better looking). She was well provided for, but doomed to loneliness.

I remember going for a picnic with two of our boarders who were sisters. It may have been on another occasion when I was in Amman, for December might have given us the wrong weather. However, it was a sunny day when a large black limousine, a Daimler, I believe, drew up and two black cloaked girls (they never wore these while at school) welcomed me into the car's spacious and comfortable depths. In front sat the chauffeur and a manservant. We drove out into the country and when we alighted, out of the boot came two beautiful Persian rugs, handsome silver and china, piles of fruit and dishes of savoury pancakes, or Arab omelettes. It was the most sumptuous picnic I have experienced, with the most perfect oriental service.

Amman, photographed in 1936

Roman Theatre in 1936, before restoration

8. Nazareth

FRAGMENT

The moonlight is blue over Nazareth
White roofs gleaming
Dark hills sleeping
Level clouds rising
Still peace brooding
The moonlight is blue over Nazareth

Boom! What was that, shattering the stillness
Tearing the darkness
Dying like thunder?
Dogs barking wildly
Startled feet running –
Who threw a bomb by moonlight in Nazareth?

'At Tantour, Nazareth' by Kathleen Hatton

On April 18th, 1940, I wrote:

"For our Easter, we had only a weekend. Now it is Easter time for the Greek Orthodox Church and the Armenians and so we are having our proper Easter holidays. I have come here with Eileen Fenton for a few days. Fortunately, fares are cheap in Palestine and hostels (or hospices) also take us for a reasonable sum. The country all around here is very beautiful and it is high and not too hot. We are wearing our summer clothes now and it is unlikely that there will be any more rain before November. Yesterday, we saw the well where Mary used to draw her water, and the house where Jesus lived."

The well is often called the Virgin's Fountain. To see the women in their native dress and veils drawing their water is to feel oneself back in Biblical times but often, by the 1940's, they no longer carried the water in the earthenware pots that complete a picture; instead they used 'tannekies', empty square-topped oil tins, about which one could weave no romantic thoughts.

'The house where Jesus lived' is also unconvincing. Again, in the 1940's, beneath the Franciscan Monastery of the Holy Ground, there were several caves, said to have been the dwelling places of the Holy Family and place of the Annunciation. Now, I believe, these are mostly covered by the Great

Basilica of the Annunciation built in 1965. It is now the biggest and richest church in the Middle East, as perhaps it should be, as Nazareth might be called the birthplace of Christianity and it is now an almost completely Christian town. Almost all denominations are represented there and there are many churches. One, of particular interest perhaps, is the Greek Catholic Church, erected in 1741 over a very old synagogue, where it has been said that Jesus learned his alphabet and where he preached "The Spirit of the Lord is Upon Me", so angering the Jews that they threatened to throw him over the hill now known as the Hill of Precipitation. Near this hill there is a Franciscan Church, known as the Church of Our Lady in Fright. It is said to be where Mary stood in fear when she thought they were going to throw Jesus to his death. What many of us remember most from this whole situation is that "a Prophet is not without honour except in his own country."

At Mary's Well, Nazareth

I do not remember a great deal from my sight-seeing in Nazareth, except the Biblical feeling of the fountain, the Souk, a street of Eastern shops with many eastern figures walking there and above all the surrounding hills. There is a church dedicated to the Boy-Jesus (sometimes now called the Church of Jesus the Boy or Jesus-Adolescent.) To get there, one has to climb a winding stony path. It is easy to imagine Jesus climbing such a path to the hill-tops, gazing on the country roundabout, looking towards Carmel or snow-clad Hermon, or Tabor (now called the Mount of Transfiguration) or the old capital of Galilee Sepphoris (or Zipporian).

Sepphoris, by 1940, was an insignificant village and Nazareth had become the 'capital' of Galilee. Whenever I went to Nazareth, I loved climbing up the stony paths to the hill-tops to enjoy the view and above all, perhaps, to revel in the tiny jewel-like flowers beneath my feet. I would lie among them, and even pick a few, my Jesus flowers. I would dream my dreams and renew my spirit where I feel sure Jesus rested and visions came to Him.

On that first visit to Nazareth, I would descend the hill, leaping down the hillside, my appetite increasing for a good French meal. Our hospice was run by the nuns of the order of St. Vincent de Paul. They all looked beautiful and moved elegantly, with French grace. Their head-dresses were wonderful, starched and white and enormous, with 'wings' of birds, or boats, or angels. (I have heard the Sydney Opera House likened to birds or boats, but I have often thought of the nuns of St. Vincent de Paul as a comparison).

Shopping in Nazareth in the 1940s.

Eileen and I looked forward to a little company at meal times, but were disappointed. Often, we had none; occasionally one little fair-haired chap came in. He was almost speechless. We were told he was a Polish refugee, knew very little English and was convalescing after a serious illness. We discovered, however, that he managed to climb the hills and painted up there. We saw him with his artist's boards under his arm. When not out, he listened to the wireless in a tucked-away, secluded room. He needed the quiet, we were told. We did not really think much about him, except that taciturn, laconic meal companions can be a little embarrassing. You do not know whether to draw them in or leave them out.

The day before we left, we saw the young man descending the hill rapidly and thought he must be recovering his health.

A few days afterwards, we heard that the very day we left, the army police had arrived and arrested him. He was no Pole, but a German spy. No wonder he had said little at meal times. It was his business to listen and see if we gave anything away. We decided we had known nothing; could not have said anything that could have been of use to him. We also decided that his art work had been the mapping of the district. Megiddo was not so far away; the site of decisive battles from Solomon BC to Allenby in 1917. We did just wonder about Vichy French?

A Wedding in Nazareth

Later on, when I was living in Haifa, I had a wonderful visit to Nazareth. An Arab friend I had made on the staff of the English High School invited me to go to the wedding of a relative of hers.

Whether Joseph or Jesus were carpenters we do not know for certain, although it is often assumed so. Tekton, the Greek word translated 'carpenter', has the broader connotation of 'workman' and it is possible that Joseph was employed in the wider field of the building trade, or so I have seen argued. The humble poverty of Jesus' earthly family is also argued, but we must remember that St. Paul, a man of learning and good standing, was also a tent-maker. Manual labour was practised alongside intellectual accomplishment. (Perhaps this long tradition as ancestral memory made it easier for refugee doctors, lawyers and other professionals to become bus drivers and manual workers when they came to refuge in Palestine).

I am digressing from the wedding. I remember clearly arriving at a happy house; I think it was that of the bridegroom's family. There were many women preparing food, beating meat rhythmically pounding spices, stopping to whirl a friend in a little dance with a cooking implement perhaps in one hand, keeping time and ululating joyfully all the time. The results of their cooking were deliciously tasty.

Later in the day, friends of the bridegroom arrived and he appeared as from nowhere and was lifted into a 'barber's chair' and out on a roof-top they proceeded to shave him, amidst much merriment. Finally, they bore him off somewhere.

Soon then, we women set out for the bride's home. I was always fascinated by the contrasts and incongruities one found in the Holy Land: often old and new, East and West walked side by side.

As the wedding party began to climb the sandy, stony winding path up the hillside, I felt the fashionable modern dresses and high-heeled slingback shoes did not quite fit the background. My shoes were a little more 'sensible' and no doubt a good deal more comfortable. We each carried a lamp as dusk was approaching. We were the wise maidens who had (I hoped) all the oil we needed in our lamps – this was an age-old custom recorded in the New Testament. We had not too far to go and our feet and our lamps lasted us. We were warmly welcomed and soon off our feet and sitting comfortably ensconced round three sides of a large room. On the fourth side, there was a kind of throne and soon the bride-to-be was occupying it. There was some singing (of an ululating kind) and different people added lines to the words, commenting on the happy situation – a practice rather like that which created ballads of the past. Large candles were lit and carried round as the bride rose and glided or danced round the room displaying her dress to advantage. Then she left us and we were handed 'small-eats'. She returned in another dress. This circulation was repeated several times and each time she ended by stamping on the light of a candle – to put an end to any evil spirits that might threaten her marriage, I was told. Was this the main purpose of the ritual, or was it the very up-to-the-minute dance to display the riches of her trousseau? Each dress seemed to be more glamorous than the one before until the evening drew near its close, with her sitting regally again in her very best. Then we heard cries in the distance. I heard then that this heralded the approach of the bridegroom. "Behold the bridegroom cometh".

I don't think he actually arrived that night. It was just the sign for our departure. The next day, the nuptials were solemnised in a Greek Orthodox Church. I remember best the moment of solemn vows when bride and bridegroom knelt before the richly robed priest and crowns were held over their heads. It was their day; they reigned supreme.

Weddings in Jerusalem

Greatly in contrast to that Arab wedding of which I wrote, which took place in an ancient Nazareth church with ancient customs, was another I attended soon after I went to live in Haifa.

A few weeks after I arrived in Jerusalem, Marion Gilmour arrived from Scotland to teach modern languages at Jerusalem Girls' College. Later, she transferred to a post in the Secretariat, where her languages were of more use to the war effort. She then went to live in the Scottish Hospice, a very comfortable and well-run place to stay. There she met Dennis Small, an army dentist. She discovered that Dennis and I had already met; we had been at Liverpool University at the same time. So I knew and liked both of them. Now Dennis had previously lived in the Officers' Mess at Allenby Barracks. There he had become friendly with Frank Gidney, who was, like Marion, a graduate of Glasgow University. Dennis and Marion became engaged and they asked me to be bridesmaid and Frank to be Best Man. Their wedding took place in November 1943 in St. Andrew's Scots (Presbyterian) Church, only 17 years old. I have always thought it an architectural triumph. Church and Hospice are beautifully unified and entirely compatible with their site, looking across the Hinnom Valley towards Mount Zion. The church is modern of its times, but reflecting ancient local architectural tradition. Inside, it is simple, plain even, but well-lit and comfortable! The seats were each given by a different parish in Scotland and the donor is named on a small metal plaque attached. The church was built as a thanksgiving for the deliverance of the Holy Land from Turkish rule and as a memorial to the Scots who died in that deliverance. The foundation stone was laid by Field Marshall Viscount Allenby, who had proudly led the troops on foot into Jerusalem in 1917. The architect was Clifford Holliday, whose interest in Armenian monastic architecture is well reflected in his design.

St. Andrew's Church (Scots Presbyterian)

The wedding was a typical war-time wedding, the men in uniform, the bride and I in short useful-again dresses, hers blue, mine dusky pink. The 'bride's mother' was the Lady Warden of the Hospice and the Jerusalem Head Post Master led her into the church.

The reception was held in the Hospice. Frank was greatly praised for his speech. One lady guest said to me afterwards, "Did you know the Best Man? That was the best wedding speech I have ever heard." I had never met Frank Gidney till that day. I was to get to know him well later. We eventually married.

The Minister who conducted Dennis' and Marion's marriage was a very solemn gentleman. Someone said to Frank, "If he is as solemn as that at a wedding, what can he be like at a funeral?" Nevertheless, it was a very happy occasion, with the background of war far from our minds.

JERUSALEM WEDDING

The wedding took place yesterday at St. Andrew's Church, Jerusalem, between Captain D.H. Small, Army Dental Corps, of Southport, Lancashire, and Miss Marion Watson Gilmour, of Inchinnan, Renfrewshire. The ceremony was performed by Rev. Duncan MacGillivray.

Lt. F.R. Gidney, R.A. was groomsman and the maid of honour was Miss Elizabeth Bushell. The bride was given away by Mr. D.H. Mackay.

Among the guests at the reception given by Mrs. MacRae at St Andrew's Hospice were Brig. J.W.C. Stubbs, DSO, MC; the Rev. and Mrs. Semple; Mr. J. Gutch; Mr. and Mrs. Badcocks; Major J. Nicholl, MBE; and members of the Station Officers Mess, Jerusalem; Major H. Betts M.B.E.; and Major P.G.D. Sixsmith.

Elizabeth

Frank

Another wedding (of a senior Padre) took place in Jerusalem while I was there. It was a white wedding at St. George's Anglican Cathedral.

One of the most intriguing photographs in my Palestine collection is that of a camel kneeling outside the entrance to the Cathedral. His position is almost prayerful. He has raised his head as if evoking the Almighty. His mouth is open in exaltation with the wedding march? Or is he patiently, or impatiently, waiting for the ceremony to be over? Is he expressing hurt feelings that nobody has invited him in? Is he the only uninvited guest? How did he come to be there in the first place? Who brought him or whom did he bring? Somewhere in the back of my mind, I seem to remember tales of an age-old custom that it was lucky for the bridegroom to come to his wedding on a camel, but I cannot imagine this bridegroom, a senior army chaplain immaculate in dress uniform, arriving on the camel. Is he proud to be at the wedding? He looks lordly. Did he bring some emir or caliph?

The Camel Who Came to the Wedding

The camel is always lofty and enigmatic. I only hope that, after the wedding, when it comes to drinking health they don't forget to invite the camel to join them. He is probably a good Moslem and will not want Champagne, only a good, long drink of water.

The Wedding in St. George's Anglican Cathedral

9. Ain Karim

I will show you –
Some of the things that were long ago done
Take heart. Make perfect your will
Let me show you the work of the humble.

The only wisdom we can hope to acquire
Is the wisdom of humility: humility is endless.

What life have you if you have not life together?
There is no life that is not in community
And no community not lived in praise of God.
T.S. Eliot – Burnt Norton, East Coker and The Rock

Of all the places that I got to know in Palestine, I think Ain Karim was my favourite. I visited it often, staying there sometimes for several weeks. It came nearest to being my *home* in Palestine. To go there was to rest, to shed one's cares, to enjoy beauty, quietness, friendliness and a spiritual simplicity and grace. One became sensible of a long link with Biblical history and a new awareness of the communion with the saints.

I first travelled to Ain Karim, about three miles from Jerusalem, on a rickety old grey bus. When we got off, there was the 'gracious fountain' in front of us, or the Virgin's Well, as some called it, for there Mary may have drawn water. Nearby, I immediately noticed and exulted in a small Mimosa tree. I had not seen one before and I rejoiced in the discovery of the soft and gentle, sweet scented, sun-reflecting flowers. At the well, one could nearly always see women gathered in their native dresses, raising water pots to shoulders or up on to their heads. It was truly age-old and Biblical, except when someone substituted for the traditional jar a tanneky, that is a petrol tin. As at Nazareth, this modern substitution always left me rather disturbed, although I suppose it was a practical change.

I spent time at Ain Karim with many different people and I stayed in three different buildings.

Let me digress for a moment to talk of coincidences, which always fascinate me. I found, when I went to Jerusalem, that there were already there two people with whom I had previously had a connection. One was Zena Wood, who had been at school with me in Canterbury. I discovered that, while I had come to teach in Jerusalem, she was already teaching in Haifa.

The other coincidence was Evelyn Cox, who was teaching Maths at J.G.C. Evelyn was the daughter of a friend of relatives of my father who lived at St. Leonard's, Hastings. I had met them briefly in the past. Both Zena and Evelyn at different times stayed with me in Ain Karim.

Ain Karim from behind the Church of the Visitation on the hillside path.

The prize coincidences of my life, however, took place some years after I left Palestine. My husband and I were on holiday travels, when we met, by chance, some girls I had taught in my first year in Jerusalem. In Venice one morning, we were breakfasting in the bright sunshine on the 'platform' built over the canal outside the Pensione Calcina, where Ruskin had written the "Stones of Venice". I looked up and saw a young woman with a baby on her arm. I thought her very beautiful, like a model for yet another artist's Madonna. I said this to my husband and then I noticed she was approaching us. She addressed me by my maiden name (I am sorry, I still do not remember her name, but I know she had married a doctor at the famous Eye Hospital of St. John, in Jerusalem).

The other similar coincidence occurred in the Souk (bazaar) in Constantinople. I was waiting to pay for some small souvenirs and Frank was looking at suede jackets, then fashionable. A smart, Arab gentleman asked him if he should buy one there or wait until they reached London. Meantime, the gentleman's wife approached the counter, looked at me and recognised me. They had come from Kuwait. Her husband said you could not help getting rich in Kuwait and she told my husband "We all loved her." – Nice to hear, even if, with true Arab courtesy, <u>all</u> might have been a slight (only slight, I hope!) exaggeration.

Both these ladies of coincidence were possibly with me at some time in Ain Karim.

The House at Ain Karim

One of my earliest visits to Ain Karim was to call on the owner of a very attractive house on the hill. She had decided that she wanted to end her days in the Holy Land. Then later, she decided to make a lengthy visit to New Zealand. She told the bishop that she wanted him and his staff to make use of her house while she was away. As a member of the Jerusalem School staff, I had the chance of renting the house from time to time, for a modest sum. As possible occasional tenants, a friend and I were invited to take tea with the owner. She proved to be quite a character, very genteel in manner, matriarchal, with a quiet daughter beside her and with a little maid who brought in a dainty tea; everything seemed to be in miniature. My friend and I confided to each other on the way back to Jerusalem that we were still rather hungry. Our youthful appetites, after some walking, told us that they preferred it when we visited Arab households, where we had been told by our hostess that we should eat as much as we liked her. (I mentioned this almost proverbial saying previously). We were expected to fill up our plates. That, also, of course, could have its disadvantages. In spite of 'can't win' situations, I still think afternoon tea is an institution worth preserving. And I am glad that I had that visit. While there, we listened to the wireless and something was announced that required a patriotic response; after a speech (was it royal or Churchillian?) the National Anthem was played. Our hostess rose to her feet and, more surprisingly, made a deep curtsey; her daughter followed her example. After a moment's hesitation and a glance at one another, my friend and I did our best to follow suit. We were unpractised in curtseying. Had our hostess lived in royal circles in her youth? Soon afterwards, the two ladies went to New Zealand for a long visit and left their house for the bishop to let as he thought fit. I was able to make good use of it, as you will read in the following pages.

Zena Wood, whom I have mentioned, was one of the first people to stay with me in Ain Karim, in the furnished house. I wrote on 4th January, 1942, "We have had a very quiet pleasant time, even quieter than we had intended, for at first it rained very hard and now everywhere is thickly covered with snow, so we have had no visitors ... Today, no buses are running and probably they won't go from the village tomorrow either." I had planned for as many as 12 girls to come, possibly for a 'Reading Party' with walks and picnics. "This time last year," I wrote, "we were doing that, but this year we have had very bad weather. It was cold and wet all over Christmas. I did not go to Bethlehem this year."

I never spent Christmas in Ain Karim, but later I will tell you of the Easter I spent there with the Russian nuns.

Ain Karim is known as the birthplace of John the Baptist, the home of Elizabeth and Zacharias, and the place of the Visitation, when Mary hurried to tell her cousin her glad news of the Annunciation. Mary dwelt for several months with Elizabeth, so that it is not inappropriate to look upon the Church of the Visitation as a shrine of motherhood. Poor Zacharias could not believe that his wife, no longer young, could be about to bear a child. We are told that, for his disbelief, he was struck dumb until the time of naming his son, John. (Hard on him, I think!)

The whole of this Ain Karim story is told with beautiful simplicity at the beginning of St. Luke's gospel. It gives us two of the most moving canticles that have been sung in our churches through the ages, the Magnificat of Mary and the Benedictus that Zacharias uttered when his speech was restored to him. (Not long after, in the Gospel, when Jesus is presented in the Temple Simeon, taking up the Holy Child, utters the short Nunce Dimitus, perhaps the best loved religious song of all).

There were churches in Ain Karim in Byzantine and in Crusader times. The Crusaders spoke of 'The Church of St. John in the Mountains', an attractive name. Since Ain Karim village lies in a valley between surrounding hills, the Church of St. John, said to be built over the site of the home of Zacharias, is within the village and near to hills on one side, while the Church of the Visitation is on the opposite hillside. Many times, I climbed the hill path past the Church of the Visitation and on upward to the Russian Convent or to the Hospice and Shrine of Peace. Having left Mary's

Well behind, I began to feel particularly the other-worldly atmosphere of Ain Karim as I passed the tower and the entrance to the Visitation church. On its façade, Elizabeth is portrayed in a delicately coloured mosaic greeting Mary. At that point, I felt a kind of greeting too. The Church was not finished till 1946, so I never saw it completed. Usually, I was making my way higher up the hill to the compound of the Russian nuns.

Sometimes, I went up higher to gain a view from the top. There, one day, I discovered that I was not sitting on grass, but on a grass-covered stone. There were several such stones, we found. We learnt that we had 'discovered' the foundations of a Russian Cathedral that had never been built, because the Revolution came. How magnificent a Russian Cathedral would have been on that hill-top, something like the Church of St. Mary in Gethsemane, with golden domes and crosses radiant in the sunshine.

Let us now come down the hill a little, to the Russian Convent. I remember that where I lived in Kent as a young schoolgirl, there was an Ursuline convent. At one time, I nearly went to school there, although I was Anglican, not Roman Catholic.

The Nuns' Market Morning – Ain Karim – An Impression

The convent was very cut off from local life; a large, rather forbidding red brick building behind high walls, topped with broken glass. How different was the Russian Orthodox Convent in Ain Karim. It was more like a miniature village. Each nun had her own little white house. In the centre was a little church, in front of which there was, above a few steps, a paved square where the nuns brought something to sell to one another of the few vegetables they had grown in their tiny gardens. A Victorian type street lamp stood at one side, adding to the picturesque scene of this small market place. I wish I had a photograph of the dark grey figures of the nuns in their working clothes standing, kneeling, sitting or squatting as they laid out their meagre stock or gathered it up disconsolately if it did not sell, as well it might not, for it was likely that all grew much the same produce. More or less opposite the square stood the Pilgrim House. Before the war, many pilgrims had come from Russia by boat, landing at Jaffa and then coming to stay, some at Ain Karim, some at the other Russian Convent on the Mount of Olives. Looked at from the opposite hillside or from the village, the Convent area looked most inviting. In a letter home I said, "The compound is very beautifully planted with pine trees and cypresses, with pale grey-leafed olives and pink-flowered oleanders. It is extremely quiet and just the place for a really peaceful holiday." I expect that, in the past, peace was often broken by the multitude of pilgrims who descended upon it. I am afraid that we also sometimes disturbed the peace a little.

One year, Sirapi Ohanessian, one of our Armenian staff, arranged for us to rent one of the little cottages, but when we arrived with our gear, we found that the nun who normally lived there had no intention of moving out. She would share it with us. Sirapi said this was quite impossible: the accommodation was inadequate and the two 'life-styles' would not agree. So Sirapi, who spoke Arabic, went and argued the situation. Eventually, the Mother Superior became involved and she solved the predicament by offering us the Pilgrim House instead. This was greatly to our advantage. It was much more spacious, in fact it was rather like a village hall, with a kitchen and other rooms opening off it. The arrangement was so satisfactory, that we went there more than once. It was large enough for four of us to go together and to have a number of visitors. The beds were hard, very hard, not just nunnery hard, but penitentially hard, but being young, we soon got used to them – good for us, probably! When pilgrims slept there, I think they just piled up on the floor! Cooking was a bit of a problem, just one primus stove, but the weather was hot and cold meals were what we wanted most.

I have mentioned that we sometimes rather disturbed the peace. One of my letters gives some idea of how it happened.

"One of the great joys of having this house has been that we could have visitors so much more easily than at school. On several occasions, we have had girls who had just left school and three of them camped here for the night. They thought it great fun and we really enjoyed having them."

One day, we had an At Home for senior girls and they came in their hordes, great streams of them winding their way up the hill between 3 and 4 o'clock and, I understand, completely monopolising two or three buses. There were about 40 of them in all. They all came bearing gifts; baking, sandwiches, fruit, contributions to the feast; cushions to make our wooden benches more comfortable, and one mother had kindly sent us a primus stove, as she thought two would make it easier than one: and indeed it did!

My letter says that I made kedgeree, scrambled eggs, cooked sausages and tomatoes and fish cakes, even chips!

Still on food, but with a difference – unwelcome visitors were involved! I wrote in a letter home: "My love of cats has been severely tested here. They are not the nicest inhabitants of Ain Karim. They are strays, not nice friendly strays, but horrid wild ones; they get in through open windows or anywhere they can and open cupboards and eat anything they can find, particularly the cheese. Eileen likes cheddar and a local kind and we bought on Wednesday enough to last us till we went. On Wednesday night, I had a small piece of mine. At lunchtime on Thursday, we suddenly saw a cat disappearing from the newly laid table with the rest of it in its mouth. In the evening, despite many precautions, I went in about 7 o'clock and found cupboard doors wide open and Eileen's cheese lying on the floor, half-eaten. So now we have no cheese at all – you will understand how I miss it!"

(Now, in my mellow old age, I say 'Poor cats' – and I remember that there were many poor Arabs in the village too – although Ain Karim was relatively prosperous, growing figs, bringel (eggplant), marrows, cucumbers, olives, and vines twined roundabout on the terraces. The gardens were well-watered from the 'gracious spring'. Ain Karim water is famous for its purity and it was long carried in goat skins on the backs of donkeys to supply parts of Jerusalem.

I have still not yet told you the really important things about the Russian Convent, but while I am on the subject of interruption of our pleasure, I must mention that we had one of the most serious interruptions possible. One day, we had just taken a spoonful from a strawberry jelly, when it began to wobble violently. I thought I had had a sudden attack of vertigo or the like. In an instant, though, Sirapi cried "Earthquake. Get outside!" It was a horrible sensation; a feeling of utter helplessness overwhelmed one. Almost as soon as we were all three outside, it was over; not a real quake, just a severe tremor. No great damage was done. When we went back to our luncheon table, there were some signs of disturbance. All I clearly remember is that my bookends were broken. On my 21st birthday, I had been given unusual bookends: two habited praying figures (of elegant line) in black pottery. I liked them and found them useful and decorative, holding up a few books for holiday reading. They seemed just right in their corner in the Ain Karim room. The earthquake had cut right through the taller figure. (When life and limb were sound, who could complain?) The bookends were the only 'serious' victims of our little quake. Nevertheless, I had had enough of quakes! I have never experienced another and my sympathies are profound for those caught up in one. Nature is at her cruellest in her major upheavals. No human agency can be blamed.

From feral cats and earthquakes, let me turn to our nuns. The crown of all the kindness we received in Ain Karim was the understanding of the Mother Superior. I wrote home; "The Abbess here has done everything she could for us. We enjoy visiting her very much, although she speaks mainly Russian and Arabic. One of the sisters knows English well and so she often translates for us. She is an interesting person who has lived in many different countries." It was these two dear ladies whom we got to know best, although we always enjoyed the kindly gentleness of all the nuns. At that time, almost all the members of the community were Russian, although there were a few young Arabs, orphans I believe, whom they were training as novices. (I have heard in more recent times that all the Ain Karim nuns are now Arabs).

The nuns had been 'caught' in Palestine at the time of the Revolution in 1917. The Russian Orthodox Church had, at one time, been rich, but the Soviet Government appropriated most of their wealth. Our nuns lived on 70 Palestine piastres a month for food and clothing (less that 15 shillings [75p], though, as usual, we have to make some allowance for the general change in money values, of which I may say a little more later). Their means were very, very meagre.

A Russian nun

There were about 150 nuns in the compound in the early 1940's. We visited only a few of them. We could almost get lost along the meandering paths of what was virtually a village. We usually waited till someone invited us in to her little cottage, whitewashed outside and in, then enjoyed finding our way back through the 'maze'. In each room of each cottage, there was an icon and whenever the sister went in or out of her room, she bowed and crossed herself before the holy 'companion' of her otherwise lonely home.

On visiting Reverend Mother, it was the custom for a nun to say the 'Kyrie Eleison' (Lord have mercy) as a blessing before knocking for entrance. I feel it would have been nice if we had done the same. In Reverend Mother's small domain, there were icons, pictures of a Russian village (perhaps the one which she would have called 'home') and of Ain Karim itself. Above all, we were surprised to see the pride of place given to the Tsar and Tsarina. The nuns seemed unable to believe in any assassination and looked forward to the restoration of the Tsar when the war was over.

I have told you of the morning market on the cobbled pavement outside their little church. Much of their day would then be taken up in household chores and keeping their village neat and tidy. The day would be punctuated by prayer, some times of recreation and meeting each other and then, as light faded, in their best black habits and peaked veils, they would light their lanterns and go forth to meet their bridegroom, their Lord, in evening prayer. This is delightful to see and the daily high point in their lives, which radiate a simple joy.

I must tell you of two important annual celebrations which these dear souls had. One is the coming of Mary. This takes place three days after the Feast of the Assumption. An icon of Mary is brought from the Russian Cathedral in Jerusalem to stay for 3 months with the nuns in Ain Karim. Her return journey takes place on the Feast of St. John, the Forerunner. To the nuns, this is a very personal thing and they even weep when Mary leaves them. There is a naïve sweetness in such joy and sorrow.

The great occasion of the year is Easter, preceded by a ceremony of confessions one to another on the first day of Lent. I was privileged to spend one Easter at Ain Karim and share in their main service and the feast that followed it. Their little church has many icons which they kiss reverently after adorning them with little gifts and flowers. Easter is one of the occasions when they all partake of the eucharistic elements, the bread being dipped in the wine (a custom which arose, it is said, to decrease the movement among the large congregations that could cause spillage of the holy blood, the wine from the chalice).

I remember a great Bible being brought forward early in the service (written in Cyrillic script) and read in a deep intoning voice by one of the leading sisters, Sister Xania. At the end of the service, there were joyous cries of "Christos aneste!" – Christ is risen. Everyone repeated it and Easter kisses were exchanged as we moved from the church, now well-lit by many candles, to a large room where Easter breakfast was set out. We ate delicious home-made bread and partook of hard boiled eggs, dyed and painted, as of Fabergé, and best of all, each nun rejoiced to see before her place a tin of Libby's Evaporated milk! That seemed to be the best thing of all to them. One could not help loving them for their almost childlike joy over simple things. I think, above all, Ain Karim gave me a realisation of how precious is this capacity for sincere and unaffected joy in simple things. It also carried me through many years of public hatred of Russian communism. I always knew that Russia must have many ordinary lovable people and admirable people and people who created wonderful art.

I have already expressed some appreciation of the Abbess. She, like most of her nuns, came of peasant stock, but she was typical of people everywhere and at all times, born with such gifts that they lead the way with dignity and natural authority, to the benefit of others.

Sister Xania could be described as her right-hand woman. She was a well-educated woman, knowing several languages, able to translate for the Abbess and enact business with government authorities. She had a delightful little weakness for excursions, for instance, to collect sugar for the convent bees. I do not understand bee-keeping, but that was one thing in which sister Xania seemed to be an expert. She was also an expert painter of icons. I wanted to buy one from her but, at that time, she had only one of St. George available. In spite of my admiration for our soldier saint, I never much liked his dragon, even if one regarded it as merely symbolic of evil. Later, I learnt that dragons and earthquakes were more or less equated. Did St. George deliver Ain Karim from an earthquake in some way? If I had known, I would have accepted his fiery dragon as representing earth's eruptions. I let my chance slip and have always regretted not having a Sister Xania icon.

As a young woman, Sister Xania had been married to an engineer. They fled Russia at the time of the Revolution, going to Finland and then Geneva. After her husband died, she decided to become a nun in Palestine, rather than in Europe. She seemed to love her little "cell" as she always called her cottage. She had a learned row of books on her shelves, a wealth of medicaments, for she acted as medical adviser to her fellow Sisters and she had her bees. She was a woman of great charm and humility, which made her able to be a most useful and well-loved member of her community.

I cannot leave Ain Karim without telling you of the most lovable of all the Redoubtable Ladies. Ain Karim was the domain of Miss Carey during the Mandate years. The first time I went to the village on my own, as soon as I alighted from the bus, an Arab came up to me and said "Miskeri". After a moment, I smiled, as understanding dawned. He wanted to show me the way to Miss Carey's house and hospice. His smile broadened and in Arabic, he told me what a wonderful lady she was, how much she had done for the village, setting up looms for weaving and other schemes for their employment, and they all loved her. I could not have understood all this if I had not already heard it told in English. He had some eggs for Miss Carey, so we climbed the hill together and when he had finished his Salaams and handed over the eggs, he returned happily to the village and I was warmly welcomed to the house.

There was something almost fey about Miss Carey, too good for this world, and yet she obviously had a good business head and a capability for organising. She had a strong faith in God, and in humankind. I remember once, when I was staying in the Pilgrim House, receiving a visit from her. She suggested that we go out together and visit somewhere. I took the large door key with me and, as I was locking the door, she asked me why I did that. She said, quite firmly "You don't need to do that, you know." I believe she had forgotten how to lock doors. Usually, Miss Carey, who came from Guernsey, was dressed in old-fashioned, country village style (she might almost have been the prototype of Miss Marple!). But in the evening, she blossomed. She had a lovely Bethlehem type dress, beautifully embroidered in a traditional design. Later, she had an assistant, younger, prettier I suppose, with golden hair and blue eyes and this lady also took to wearing a local dress in the evening. I remember, however, with some regret, that her dress was embroidered in flowers in lazy daisy stitch. Some things should not be modernised, some traditions not exported.

It was wonderfully restful to sit in deck chairs and enjoy tea in Miss Carey's garden and perhaps meet there other people, mostly of the missionary fraternity, from all over the Near East. Miss Carey was not only Lady Bountiful to the village, but also the provider of a holiday refuge to many expatriates of small means. She was also providing for the future, almost for an apocalyptical or escatological future. In her garden she had built a little chapel, a Shrine of Peace, where Christians, Jews and Moslems could all go and pray for peace and reconciliation. She had had woven a royal blue carpet with crosses, the Star of David and the Islamic Crescent in its design. I think this may be better appreciated now than then. Some Christians felt it wrong to 'equate' the religions in this way. Certainly, all people were welcome at Miss Carey's and they knew that and they often came. Miss Carey also looked to the future in willing her property to the Anglo-Catholic Sisters of the Love of God. She hoped they would come to Ain Karim and carry on one day, where she left off.

Eventually, Miss Carey had to give up and return to Britain. Shortly before her death, I received a card from her. There was a picture of angels on one side and, on the other side, she wrote as if she were already in heaven with the angels. They talk of people being 'away with the fairies', but Miss Carey, quite rightly, was 'away with the angels'. I am sure they would welcome her as she used to welcome us.

I have read recently that Ain Karim has been greatly 'developed'. There are extensive hospital buildings on the hill, a building which is too obtrusive, some think. (I wonder if it is where the Russians once laid the foundations of a cathedral before 1917, or is it a worthy successor to the visions of Miss Carey?)

10. Kibbutzim

From the tirelessness and the other-worldly atmosphere of Ain Karim, I turn to modernity and community life of quite a different kind. During April, 1942, I spent four days walking with three Jewish girls in the north of Palestine, Mary, Annelise and Ruth. It was at their suggestion, request or invitation, but I felt I had some responsibility for them, especially as, prior to our departure, I was invited to visit the Tel-Aviv home of the guardian of one of them. I soon realised that this was a little more than a social visit: I was being vetted, and then I was asked to see that they did nothing foolish. On returning, my only comment on this holiday expedition was: "We spent almost nothing on the trip, as each night we stayed in a Jewish colony. These communal settlements are very hospitable and, though what they offer is simple and sometimes surprising, they charge nothing and are very kind." The 'colonies were, of course, the newly formed kibbutzim.

I will tell you first about some of the 'surprises'. One came on the very first night. I had been assured that we did not need to book: we would always be taken in. So it proved. We were welcomed, fed, invited to watch some dancing and then to join in. The dances were mostly 'circular', with some singing and shouting. All this went on in a barely furnished, wooden-floored hut. It turned out that this was also to be our bedroom. After walking and dancing (or trying to!), I was almost dropping where I stood with tiredness. And that is exactly what we were expected to do – and virtually what we did. There was no being a starched English school-ma'am. Equality was a basic principle of Kibbutz life. I can't remember much about washing that night. But the second day, after traversing some beautiful countryside and sleeping on a paliasse on a kind of shelf, I found that all means of washing or bathing were entirely communal. The next night, at our second Kibbutz, it was again some form of harsh straw mattress. By this time, I thought I was ready for sleeping on a tight-rope, as it is said. The main thing was, I SLEPT. Such is the adaptability of youth. (Compared with Kibbutzim, Ain Karim of the convent was luxury indeed). On our final night, we visited one of the earliest founded settlements. It was still simple, but not <u>so</u> simple. Then came another 'surprise'. Sleeping was communal for unmarried people. We were shown into a mixed dormitory. Well, I suppose if we didn't undress it would be rather like the war-time experience of 'dossing down' in an improvised London underground air-raid shelter. (Of course, now one's mind would immediately think of the co-ed wards – or 'stations' – in some hospitals. The girls whom I was with, and for whom I felt in some measure responsible, were very anxious to fit in. 'When in Rome' half of me said ('though how different from Rome). Then I thought of the caring guardian who had 'interviewed' me. I braced myself and said, "Please, can we have rooms to ourselves?" So we were given two small rooms with two BEDS and two little truckle beds. The girls explained that I was English: that always explained any oddity of behaviour, and met with an indulgent smile.

This older and larger Kibbutz had its own fishponds. It may have been the oldest Kibbutz, Degania. It was not far from the Lake of Galilee and we had Peter fish and fish salads and more fish. But the food, in its own way, was good. It would have delighted nutritionists of today (1998).

Mary and Annelise lending a hand at the Kibbutz.

Everybody in the community had a job contributing to the general welfare. They aimed to be entirely self-supporting – cooking, cleaning, working the land, looking after cattle, making clothes, administering, running a clinic, educating the children. Private property did not exist and privacy was almost non-existent. Married people had one room and saw their children for only a short part of the day: otherwise the young were in a kind of crèche. There was basically a law of the land. They would work long hours to develop and beautify it. People were of all ages, all 'classes' (to use our familiar term), all kinds of abilities and occupations. Decisions were taken by majority vote. They had one thing in common. They had *escaped* and they were *free*.

My picture of Kibbutz life is a rather smudgy one, so here is a brief note to clarify the ideas behind the settlement scheme.

These notes are based on a condensed version of information in an Israeli guide book. They mention nothing about 'escape' or freedom. As well as refugees, local Jews and Jews from the diaspora in American and European countries joined the movement more frequently as time went on, with patriotic and idealistic aims.

"A Kibbutz is a work orientated place" and one must contribute by working hard. Working on the land is of great importance. Children are given 'the best of everything' and are brought up to carry on the kind of life into which they have been born. Little privacy and no private property. Money is provided for "clothes, books, a radio, a watch." Each person gets living quarters, stationery, stamps, newspapers, medical services --a Marxist democracy. Degania, the first Kibbutz, was founded in 1909 by young Russian immigrants. Within 50 years, about 200 were founded.

They originally grew out of reaction against old Orthodoxy. Then came social and economic equality and the need for group security. Then the 'back to the land' mystique prevailed – with wonderful results in expert growing of citrus fruit, tree planting, etc. Later, many came off the land into their own factories and a commercial element entered in.

Later still, some left the protected life where everything was cared for, taking with them some of the ideals into the wider community. Among other changes was the growth of good hospices, where even tourists could stay very comfortably.

The other day, I read that so many are now seeking the wider life that the Kibbutzim are in danger of disappearing.[2] Perhaps as their century draws near, they will no longer exist – certainly not as they were once experienced. I think I experienced 'the real thing'!

We must have spent a second night in this last Kibbutz, for I remember clearly climbing mount Tabor by moonlight – a wonderful clear, starry night – and arriving at the summit in time to see dawn and sunrise, for me a New Transfiguration. Two – or was it three? – young men from the Kibbutz suggested the expedition and escorted us. It was nice to be hosted in this way. It was a good choice, for the significance of the site; the church of the Transfiguration for me and the association with Deborah and Barak for the Jews. In ancient times, Tabor was always a Holy Mountain. Deborah's song after the fall of Sisera is one of the finest passages of poetry in the Old Testament. At the end of it, there is a perhaps unintended passage of great pathos: the mother of the defeated looks in vain for the return of her son:

> *Out of the window she peered*
> *The mother of Sisera gazed through the lattice.*
> *Why is his chariot so long in coming?*
>
> *Her wisest ladies make answer*
> *Nay, she gives answer to herself*
> *She had been imagining triumph*
> *Are they not finding and dividing the spoil?*
>
> *Spoil of dyed stuffs for Sisera*
> *Spoil of dyed stuffs embroidered*
> *Two pieces of dyed work embroidered*
> *For my neck as spoil?"*

What kind of woman is she? Selfish, vain... Then Deborah ends.

---

[2] In 2011 the Kibbutzim have now disappeared.

"So perish all Thine enemies, O Lord!"
What do we think at this point? Then –
"But Thy friends be like the sun as
He rises in His might."

Those last lines befitted our climb perfectly, and those with me were my friends. I saw the outside of the church, pink and golden as the sun rose. It had been mysterious and mystic by moonlight. Then the spirit gave way to the body. We were hot and thirsty. A monk came out from the monastery, an American, to my surprise, (but it was American Catholics who financed the gleaming Basilica in the 1920's). We were given cooling drinks. Whether breakfast was from the refectory or from a hop-sack, I cannot remember. What I can remember is the wonderful situation (2000 feet above the Mediterranean), looking out across the plain of Esdralon towards Galilee; fertile land with nearby cypresses and graceful trees and, fairly near, ruins of a Benedictine Abbey, a few dwellings and the picturesque old Greek church of St. Elias.

Church of the Transfiguration Mount Tabor

The climb to the top had been arduous. I have seen the approach described as a zig-zagging golden thread. (A reminder of the golden strings of my golden ball was not inappropriate.) In the ninth century, 4,340 steps had been cut for pilgrims to get to the summit. I think I stumbled up some of those old steps! Going down, of course, was much easier, but as the sun was up we got much hotter.

Some scholars, probably the majority, now think that the Transfiguration must have taken place at a certain point on Mount Hermon, but I prefer to think it took place on Mount Tabor – having made that climb and seen that transfiguring sunrise.

11. Galilee

O Sabbath rest by Galilee
O calm of hills above.
  TRIOLET

Suddenly, Hermon was there,
Shouting "O Sleeper, awake!"
As we rounded the hill unaware
Suddenly Hermon was there,
Flinging her snows to the air,
Over the mist-blue lake.
Victorious, Hermon was there
Crying, "O Sleepers, awake!"
  Kathleen Hatton

Hermon dominates in Galilee, in Lebanon – and over Haifa Bay.

Galilee – "Always Hermon was there". Oleanders on the shore.

I enjoyed the calm and the rest of Galilee several times. Neither the restless night in Tiberias, nor the thrilling moonlight and sunrise on Thabor meant as much to me as the quiet and peace of that lovely lakeside (whether you call it Lake Tiberias, Chennereth, Genassereth or Galilee). Many people visiting Galilee during the war years (of which I must remind you I am writing) would stay at Tabgha. I had only one short visit to Tabgha to see the famous mosaics which had only been discovered in 1932. Tabga is a shortened form of Heptapego, meaning Seven Fountains and there are seven springs in the small lush green valley, one of which is hot and health-giving. A tiny church stands some way in from the shore, where a much older church once stood still farther from the shore and where, beneath concrete walls and corrugated iron roofs may be found most delightful mosaics of the fourth century stretching over an apse and nave of the one-time Byzantine Church. These mosaics should be a Mecca for all nature lovers and wild life charities! The artist obviously loved and understood the ways and the spirit, particularly of birds. The mosaics have in them little houses with conical roofs – no people. (Was there some Moslem influence– or should I say Semitic influence– behind this?)

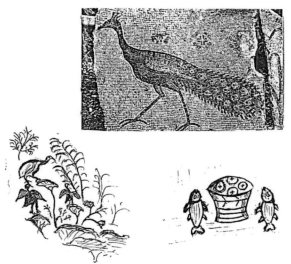

Mosaics in the Church of the Loaves and Fishes

What lovely contrasts we have: I know that there are icon-filled churches where good souls find a real communion with the saints represented, how nice to be reminded that there is a restfulness and an uplifting of the spirit in contemplating the forms of 'natural' creation. Go and see, if you can, the Tabgha birds and flowers (one tiny bird perched on a flower bell) of birds preening themselves and ruffling their feathers and an ornamental snake and quite a natural badger. I think the artist got carried away by his love of nature for the main motif and theme is the miracle of the loaves and fishes.

What of Nature in reality about Galilee? The nature that must have given rise to the art.

Sometimes one finds oneself in a pastoral scene where there is a shepherd with his fat-tailed sheep and long-haired goats. Sometimes, there might be Bedouin passing with a donkey or even a camel. There are trees and oleanders growing plentifully, their pink flowers and silver green leaves set off by the blue lake behind them. Sometimes, one sees a cultivated field, a golden cornfield, perhaps, or one with young green shoots; sometimes, especially near Capernaeum, there are the familiar flowers: a carpet formed of myriads of flowers, blue and yellow and some white. Nestling where there are rocks there may be cyclamen and splashes of red anemones or ranunculi.

A Bedouin beauty

Standing by an oleander with the gently lapping water not far from her feet, I can still see a Bedouin girl in her embroidered, but dark and rather dirty dress being tugged by a much younger sister, who was shyly sucking her grubby thumb and half-turning from us and then surreptitiously looking up at us, opening her dark, dark eyes very wide, as her curiosity got the better of her. The big sister caught sight of the ring I was wearing and gestures soon indicated that she would like me to take it off and give it to her. I began to think we should move away, but she wanted to prolong the acquaintance. However, we soon parted and she beamed a farewell smile across her blue-tattooed face.

Another encounter we had on the shores of Galilee was with a youth who snatched my friend's camera and ran with it across a cultivated field. I am not sure whether she got it back or not, but I think it must be that incident which led us to a 'police station'. We found two or three young British policeman in a temporary shack (or was it only a tent?). They had been having a near *al fresco* meal. The sight of H.P. sauce on a small rickety table was a very homely touch. One felt their yearning for home and sat down and chatted about where they came from, how long they had been in Palestine, etc. while they plied us with welcome soft drinks.

Eventually, we returned to our lovely Hospice behind the Church of the Beatitudes, high on a hill overlooking the lake and surrounding countryside.

The Hospice was run by the Italian nuns of a Franciscan order. They themselves moved about with a quiet dignity and created an atmosphere of calm and peace. But we discovered that the lake was not always peaceful. It would have been nice to have had an artist's brush ever ready and the talent to make a series of paintings to show the changes of light and colour and mood, as Monet did for haystacks. We did not even have colour photography in the 1940's.

I saw the lake sparkling brilliantly blue, then with little silvery ripples passing over it and little lazy eddying fringes along its shore. I saw it turn wine-dark and indigo. I saw it change again as the moon rose above the over-shadowing mountains; the lake was overlaid with gold, which paled to a shimmering silver which gradually suffused the entire surface. One day, the lake was in angry mood. As we returned to our hill-top refuge, the caressing air grew cooler and the colour all around us changed. Soon, the lake was dark chrome and brooding, a wind lashed its waters, a sinister yellow light enveloped everything. The waters became a ghastly tawny ochre and lightning flashed frighteningly over them, cutting deep, you felt, beneath the surface. Then "Calm, be still" came almost as suddenly. I have seldom seen Nature so alarmingly dramatic.

The Church of the Beatitudes.

After that, I watched the sunrise over the tip of Hermon, a benign, pearly sky, pink, pale primrose, velvety peach and roseate it came, reflected in the waters till it was an almost forget-me-not blue, with a sea-shell lustre across it. A transformation scene indeed.

It was only a short walk from the Mount of Beatitudes to Capernaeum. I went there several times. There were flowers on the way in Springtime and the Synagogue was situated near a group of trees. Sir George Adam Smith, a scholar whom I admire, did not think that this spot now known as Tel Hum was Capernaeum, but another professor, Dalman, affirms its authenticity. There are monks at Tel Hum, more Franciscans.

Whether the synagogue, the ruins of which we now see, built in the 2nd century AD, stood on the site of the Synagogue in which Jesus preached or not, does not really matter to me. The ruins are beautiful; some elegant slender columns in the corner of a courtyard and fragments from the building beautifully carved with Jewish symbols, the Menorah (seven-branched candlestick), the Ark of the Covenant, the Shield of David and, as in the mosaic, we looked at in Tabgha, the works of nature influenced the artists who made the sculptures. We see grapes, pomegranates and swirling leaves. There are two interesting inscriptions commemorating to this day the names of men who had contributed to the building. I thought how much like us they were: in two of the most recently built churches in Jerusalem, St. Andrew's Church has names of Scottish parishes that contributed and the Church of All Nations has the names of those nations who gave likewise. Some say the original synagogue here might have been the gift of the centurion whose servant Jesus saved. Jesus came to this area after Nazareth rejected him and called Matthew from tax-collecting and Peter, Andrew, James and John to leave their fishing nets and follow him. Here, he worked miracles and, perhaps at the exact spot where we stayed, gave his new commandment – be poor in spirit; merciful, patient, pure in heart, preservers of peace, and seek the fellowship and unity of the whole human race. I think it is time to go back to the Church of the Beatitudes and pray that we may be able to fulfil this great ideal, but tremendous spiritual task. I have seen the Beatitudes described as "a code both disciplinary and transforming."

The Ruins of Capernaeum – Sculptures
Part of the Synagogue building and the vine in detail.

It was transforming to be back on the Church of Beatitudes, just to sit behind the pillared arches on the parapet surrounding the Octagonal Church, or look at a mosaic figuring a ship symbolising hope – which is perhaps the greatest anchor of life; or best of all maybe, to sit for a few minutes in the chapel before an altar which has no reredos but stands in front of a window with the lake and hills as a background. Later, I found this idea used several times in New Zealand where one could again lift up one's eyes to the hills, often more snow-clad than Hermon from Galilee.

A last walk takes us along the shore to watch the fishermen hurling their nets with poetically circular movements and drawing in a goodly catch. There is a hot spring in one part of the lake, where more than usual numbers of fish congregate. Did Jesus know this when his friends did not?

I have told you of the quietness and coolness of our Hospice. I seem to remember marble floors.

The view through the pillared arches.

You may wonder if there were many other guests. No, I do not think so; but there was a White Lady, a lovely tall elderly lady who seemed always to dress in white. I seem to remember that she claimed to be the sister of a well-known General. Was it Allenby? Had she come to spend her last years in this lovely place? At night, she always dressed for dinner in a long, white, flowing dress and after dinner she would walk in the garden. She was ethereal, mysterious and enchanting as she moved gracefully in the moonlight.

Conquering the slopes of Hermon in the snow

12. Holidays in Syria and Lebanon

In a letter dated 18th October, 1942, I wrote:

> *"I had a really marvellous holiday this year (with Peggy Craig). The first night we spent at Tiberias; it was the hottest night I remember. We had two little rooms next to each other opening on to a balcony, and opening off the balcony was our bathroom. Most of the night we were popping in and out having showers and then sitting on the balcony in the moonlight to get cool."*

I did not tell my parents in this letter that it was armies of fleas as well as heat that made the showers so necessary. Later, I read in a guidebook that the King of Fleas had his realm in Tiberias in Roman times and the Emperor Tiberias himself had been attacked as we were. We would rather not have been honoured by a 'welcome' from these royal descendants, which all the power of Rome could not conquer!

It seems that no other power through the centuries had any more success with destroying this plague. Kinglake, in the nineteenth century, suggested that every nation had made their own contribution to the continuing curse. He arrived in Tiberias late in the day and the only accommodation he could find was in one of its many churches. He did not have a holy night: he said:

> *"The congregation of fleas which attended at my church alone must have been something enormous ... The fleas of all nations were there. The smug, steady, importunate flea from Holywell Street – the pest, jumping 'puce' from hungry France – the wary, watchful 'pulce' with his poisoned stiletto – the vengeful 'pulga' of Castile with his ugly knife ' the German 'floh' with his knife and fork, insatiate, not rising from table – whole swarms from all the Russias and Asiatic hordes unnumbered – all these were there, and all rejoiced in one great international feast ... After passing a night like this, you are glad to gather up the remains of your body long, long before morning dawns."*

Since Kinglake and since Peggy and I were there, the Israelis have springcleaned and modernised Tiberias and it is now possible to advertise it as a resort boasting hot-spring baths, marinas and fashionable hotels for tourists. If they have driven out the armies of fleas, they have done a great civilising service to the Middle East!

Tiberias

After our living nightmare, we drove early the next morning along the lakeside (the Lake of Galilee or Gennaseret) to Samakh where, after waiting 1½ hours, we caught the train for Damascus. The lake was the most heavenly shimmering peacock blue; I think more lovely than I have ever seen it; and beyond the lake, Hermon gleamed in the distance, spangled with snow. The first part of the journey by train was through a gorge and, at one point, there was a thrilling waterfall; one's heart cascaded with it, for water is such a rare precious thing in this country that to see it pouring in torrents down the green and rocky mountainside was more than exciting.

At Deraa, the one junction on the way to Damascus, there were many Indian troops who (we decided from their gaze) were fascinated by my fair hair; they greatly enjoyed it when I leaned out of the carriage window and drank 'gazuz' taken from a railside vendor's goatskin 'bottle'. (I never drank that way before or since). It was for me, and not for them, I suppose, an extremely hot day and I was incredibly thirsty.

The Lake of Galilee or Gennaseret

We did not arrive in Damascus until after 10 p.m. and were very tired, but next morning, we were up early and secured a guide and did the sights, visiting the Citadel, the bazaars, the Street Called Straight, the house of Ananias, the window from which St. Paul was said to have been let down in a basket over the wall. Later, we went to a museum and several mosques, including the main one, often called the Omayyad Mosque. Although altered and restored, the building still shows that it was originally a church, the Church of John the Baptist, whose head (accepted as authentic through many centuries) is preserved in it. The Emperor Theodosius built the church in the 4th century and the Greek words of its foundation remain over one doorway. "Thy Kingdom, O Christ, is an everlasting kingdom, and thy domain endures for all generations." The church became a mosque in the 8th century, and beautiful mosaics of plants and landscapes were added. It has been said to rival the Dome of the Rock in Jerusalem as one of the wonders of Moslem art.

We also went out to a suburb to look down upon the city, with its innumerable minarets and domes and its green belt, where the river Barada flows and where the famous fruits are grown. The Barada represents the Abana and Pharphar of Biblical time, which Naaman thought much better than the Jordan, until he was cleansed of his leprosy in the Jordan. For Naaman, let me say that the waters of Damascus sparkle crystal clear and run refreshingly at the side of the streets (or so they did) while Jordan can look murky, sluggish and muddy; but for Jordan, I must say it is different at different times and in different parts; remember it flows from Galilee to the Dead Sea, and it is fed from the fresh snowy streams that come down from the glory of Hermon – and many say that Hermon was the true mountain of the Transfiguration. So may not the waters of Jordan be transfigured and capable of transfiguring? There are many rapids in its course, so it is certainly not all murky.

I cannot resist the temptation to see once more how the indomitable, aristocratic ladies of the nineteenth century found Damascus. Both Lady Hester Stanhope and Gertrude Bell entered on horseback. (One of them sometimes rode a white donkey but, wishing to impress the ruling Turks, they would both choose more noble steeds.)

Lady Hester was advised that she ought to wear a veil, but refused. "On the 31st August (1912), in the stillness of a summer afternoon, she rode with an uncovered face through the gates of Damascus." It must have been siesta time; the people who were out and saw her were spell-bound by her dignified, imperious bearing; for them, she was at once "a being apart". Pashas, Emirs, Sheiks and Caliphs all soon bowed to her will. A house had been prepared for her in the Christian quarter; but as this was the humbler part of the city, she insisted on living in the Turkish area where dwelt the high dignitaries and very soon she was provided with a palace. Soon, however, she became tired of marble courtyards and splashing fountains, receptions, coffee and sorbets and she went out among the Bedouin, in the desert lands that stretched beyond the mulberry trees and orchards of apricots. Damascus is an oasis in the Syrian desert between the spurs of the Anti-Lebanon mountain range. As in Jerusalem, one passes quickly from fruitfulness to vast emptiness of desert.

Here is Gertrude Bell's impression of Damascus. "I had a very beautiful ride into Damascus. The air was sweet with the smell of figs and vines and chestnuts; the pomegranates were in the most flaming blossom, the valley was full of mills and mill races bordered by long regiments of poplars – lovely it must be at all times, but when one comes to it out of the desert, it seems a paradise. I rode through the bazaar, eating apricots with which Damascus is full. Now he who has not eaten the apricots of Damascus has not eaten apricots." A little while later, she writes, "By the way, did I mention that Damascus is a singularly beautiful place?"

Gertrude Bell writes very naturally. Her pleasure was almost the reverse of Lady Hester's in some ways. I like her, and not quite knowing what she had already said gives me a fellow feeling.

The call of the desert has been heard by many a Westerner. T.E. Lawrence comes at once to mind, Wilfred Thesiger is another, but the call is even stronger for the Arab. Let me quote something from the translation of an Arabic poem written by the wife of a Caliph. She, like Gertrude Bell, longed to exchange her palace life for that of the desert:

> *A tent with rustling breezes cool*
> *Delights me more than palace high*
> *...*
> *The crust I ate beside my tent*
> *Was more than this fine bread to me*
> *The wind's voice where the hill path went*
> *Was more than tambour can be*
> *And more than purr of friendly cat*
> *I love the watch dog's bark to hear*

> **This poem was translated by a young officer in the 1st World War, who lost his life by drowning in the Tigris.**

What woman does not like shopping? At least when young? Gertrude Bell went off to the Damascus Bazaar on her own. She said, quite rightly, that bazaars are "the epitome of the East." We enjoyed shopping in the bazaars (the Souks). I told them at home some of the things I bought, "A beaten silver and copper plate, a tablecloth and a leather pouffe. I found the other day that I could get the pouffe stuffed for 6 piastres (1/3), so now I am enjoying sitting on it at nights when I come off duty! I also bought some leather sandals that were made for me in a funny little shop in a bazaar. They cost me three Syrian pounds, about 6/-. They are comfortable and cool." (My delight in the pouffe now surprises me!)

I cannot remember whether it was this time or on a later occasion that I experienced the cream of Eastern shopping. I walked the length of the Street Called Straight and finally came to Asfar and Sakis. (It would be an insult to say they were the Harrods of the East).

Asfar and Sakis were famous for their oriental merchandise, most famous of all for luxurious fabrics. I entered and was courteously greeted. I bought a cedarwood box inlaid with mother-of-pearl in an intricate mosaic design. Then I asked if I could see some of their celebrated silks and brocades. "Come this way, madam" – this sounded quite western in those days, when we still had elegant shop walkers in morning dress. Then, slowly, two curtains were drawn aside to reveal a hitherto hidden doorway. Beyond was a softly lit room, carpeted with rugs, scented and mysterious. Entering it was like opening a page in the Arabian nights – an Aladdin's Cave, a dwelling or a shop fit for Scheherazade. The materials were unbelievably rich in texture and design, too rich to be of use to me, I thought, but lovely to possess, like a great artist's picture. Was there one I could afford? – The simplest perhaps?

Then I began to wonder if I ought to extricate myself from temptation and just live with the memory. At that moment, coffee was offered to me by a humble employee with many salaams and almost backward retreat. I sipped the sweet Eastern coffee from its little cup. It was as if it were drugged: I was in a dream world – each silk, each damask, each brocade was lovelier than the one before it. To handle them was a delight and a privilege; one's fingers tingled with the texture and one's eyes melted before the subtlety of the colours. In the distance, I heard some faint oriental music. All the senses were brought into play. It was as if the curling smoke from a burnished lamp was clouding my mind. A second cup of coffee appeared. This brought me to the moment of decision. I chose two small pieces of soft damask silk. (No wonder Damascus gave us the words 'damask' and 'damascene'. I am sure Asfar and Sakis had some damascened swords and sword belts among their stock – but that would be another story). I paid my bill and bore away my treasures.

My husband, then quite unknown to me, also remembers Asfar and Sakis, in fact it was he who remembered the name. He had been commissioned by a friend to buy something gorgeous and luxurious for the lady he hoped to marry. What a responsibility, but at least cost did not matter to him, as it had done to me. The purchase of an exquisite brocade proved entirely satisfactory. It cemented – (what an intrusive word to use about the handling of delicate material in a delicate transaction!), I repeat, – it cemented the friendship and, more important, the courtship!

The Gateway to the Street Called Straight

The Street Called Straight. Note the pillars. Many Graceo-Roman streets were lined with pillars.

We left Damascus by car, with some acquaintances we made there by chance. Peggy's brother and a friend met us in Beyrouth and we lunched at St. George's Hotel, beautiful and beautifully situated; now gone. We then went up into the mountains, where we stayed, having a most restful and amusing time. We stayed in Brummana.[3] We were very lucky to be able to do so, for the whole area was a military zone and permission had to be granted to enter. Peggy's brother, a young Lieutenant-Colonel, had been able to get this permission for us. As a little aside, I will tell you that I was glad at this time to escape from Jerusalem for a very unexpected reason. One day, some parents visited the school (I cannot remember the function now). I met an Arab gentleman and his wife, English, I believe, and discussed their daughter's progress. Without my realising it, the husband must, like the Indians on the railway station at Deraa, have been attracted by my then golden hair, for I began getting invitations that I did not want. He even made an attempt to invade the Lebanon when he heard, somehow, that we were going to holiday there, but to my relief, he did not get the necessary permission. Whether Peggy and her brother had anything to do with this I do not know. Anyway, the episode ended there.

We had a great deal of 'military guardianship' in Brummana. On the night that we arrived at our delightful guest house, we had a dinner party

---

[3] Freya Stark called Brummana 'enchanting' and I also fell under its spell.

consisting of Peggy's brother's friends, a lieutenant, a captain, a major, Peggy's brother was the colonel and, at the head of the table, Peggy and I on either side of him, a Brigadier. Not only was the company and the conversation good (although I felt a little shy and overpowered) but the food was some of the best I have ever tasted. Lebanon used to be famous for its cuisine; Franco-Lebanese. My letter says: "Nearly every other night we had a dinner party or went out and danced." One night, I remember, we were taken to a then famous hotel higher up the mountainside, where I drank whisky for the first time and ate snails for the first and last time!

Much more delectable than snails were the lovely ripe green figs we ate at breakfast time, straight from the tree. Breakfast was served on a verandah. The sun was up, the skies sparkling and the air crisp. It was indeed good to be alive on such mornings and in such a delightful place. A letter written from Cedarhurst, Brummana, 22nd September, 1941 says: "Brummara is a most beautiful place high up in the mountains among the pines and looking over Beyrouth and St. George's Bay. The sunsets are glorious and the air is usually cool and fresh. Today, it has been cloudy and misty, which is a pleasant change from constant brilliant sunlight. We usually go for walks in the early evening when it is cool. I have spent the whole of today in the garden, reading and writing, wearing a woolly coat and wrapped up in a travelling rug (!) but greatly enjoying the air. The garden is very pretty, with many trees; we enjoy seeing so much green after the bareness of our own hills and gardens for much of the year.

Everywhere here the influence is French. The Arabs are more French in their ways than I expected they would be. The little maid who does my room is just like the lively, talkative French maids of the theatre.

As we came along, we saw some signs of war, but really very little (there had been a short Syrian campaign not long before) indeed, everything seems very peaceful, and we have heaps of delicious butter. I am looking forward to tea in the garden, with fresh rolls and butter and honey."

Lebanon before and during most of World War 2 was a place of peace and enjoyment. It is one of the areas I have been privileged to holiday in to which I would most gladly return. How lovely to see again those fruitful hills – the cedars, pines, olives, vines, mulberries, figs – and, oh, to taste those ambrosial fresh breakfast figs again.

Baalbec

Old tales of far off things, bygones of long ago whereof
*   memory still holdeth shape,*
Time and the muse have purged of their unhappiness,
with their bright broken beauty they pervade the abyss,
Peopling the solitude with gorgeous presences;
As those bare lofty columns, time whiten'd relics
Of Atlantican adoration, upstanding alone
In Baalbec or Palmyra, proudly affront the waste
And with rich thought atone the melancholy of doom

Robert Bridges: Testament of Beauty

From Brummana I was taken to Baalbec, one of the most magnificent Graeco-Roman remains in the world. I do not remember very much about the journey there. One of our army friends took me and I seem to remember that part of the way we travelled in the Post Bus. My escort saw me safely into the Baalbec Hotel and then had to proceed somewhere else on military business. I had a room overlooking the ruins so that I could see them against the dawn sky and the sunset. Six great columns, 19 metres (72 feet) high, dominate the sky. In the afternoon of my arrival, by 'army' arrangement, an Arab gentleman came to take me over to the ruins. He was the architect/archaeologist who had done much of the restoration work there. I am sorry I have no record of his name, either in memory or in letters. He was a charmingly courteous, enthusiastic and knowledgeable guide. He told me many things, too many of which I have forgotten. The city was named after the Phoenician war god Baal. Baalbec is Baal of the Bequa --Lord of the plain: the Bequa'a Valley. The Greeks called it Heliopolis. The Romans equated Jupiter with Baal and built three temples on the site, one to Jupiter, one to Bacchus (vines grow well in the Bequa'a Valley) and the third to Venus. There were 54 Corinthian columns in the Jupiter Temple, the very highest, of which only six remain. They are a magnificent landmark, reddish gold in colour; as the light plays upon them they change from deep honey colour to tawny pink or rust red. Within the precincts of the temple, many changes took place: churches (one to St. Barbara in the 13th century) and fortresses, both Christian and Moslem, were built. Villagers took away stones to build houses in time of neglect, and fire and earthquake did their worst.

More remains of the Temple of Bacchus than on the Jupiter Temple, so that it gives a better idea of its original design and beauty. The temple dedicated to Venus is a graceful round building with more slender columns.

While enjoying the ruins of Baalbec, I dropped a favourite handkerchief – a habit I have never lost! In response to my "Oh, bother!" my kindly guide showed undue concern. We searched for my jewel (like the pearl of great price) in this ancient city known to some as a jewel or a pearl itself. Our visit came to an end and I dismissed my little loss. I was to see my guide again, for he had brought with him an invitation for me to be his sister's guest at dinner. Vaguely, I think that dinner was in a Damascus hotel, although I went first to the lady's home. I remember entering her elegant bedroom and combing my hair before her mirror. I could not help enjoying the scented atmosphere and the elegant hangings and noticing, on her dressing table, more perfume bottles and exquisite cosmetic jars than I had ever seen before. Once more, the riches of the East assailed me.

The Ruins in Baalbec

There were five of us at dinner, the gentleman and lady, her daughter and a schoolfriend and I. Introduction and greetings over, I noticed a small attractive package at my place in front of me. I was invited to open it – a beautiful handkerchief, to replace the one I had lost – a far better one than that I had lost. The courtesy of the Arabs can be almost overwhelming.

A good deal of my conversation was, I think, with the two girls, both about seventeen. The school friend came from South America; Argentina? I am not sure now. They were delightful and, continuing the courtesies, gave me the compliment I always enjoyed of disbelieving that I was a schoolma'am! I was sorry not ever to be able to see four such delightful people again.

I had seen much of what the Lebanon and Syria had to offer, but I had not yet seen the famous cedars. I knew I must return to Lebanon to see them. Eventually, the opportunity came when a friend and I were invited by a 'redoubtable lady' living alone in a Lebanese village (sadly, both her name and that of her village are beyond my powers of recall, but I owe her gratitude for making a memorable experience possible).

We were up and out as dawn was breaking. The morning air was fresh and it was good to be alive and walking; we were climbing all the time on a pathway not far from a dry river-bed; it may have been the Letani (the ancient Leontes that waters the Bekka valley between Mount Lebanon and the Anti-Lebanon, two impressive ranges where snow lingers on the tops for most of the year). It is either this snow or the whiteness of the limestone rocks which gives Lebanon its name – it means white. So important were the cedars in Biblical history that the cedar tree has an honoured place on the Lebanon flag. The Greek Maronite Church refers to the cedars as the Cedars of God and, in 1843, they built a church within the forest and for long held an annual festival there. In the 1940's, about 400 trees survived. Some of them claimed to be c. 1,500 years old. They grow mainly in clumps now and can be 12 metres high and 12 metres in girth. I did not see the largest ones, nor do I know how many are surviving to the Millennium.

I remember seeing an enormous number of small cedars, but on part of our walk we saw many other lesser trees, including many pines. We picnicked near one group of cedars and were glad to see a nearby spring. By this time, it was much hotter than when we set out. We thought we would shorten our downward journey by keeping to the river-bed after we left the narrow cedars pathway. We soon found it hard work with stones underfoot and sun blazing down. I watched my left arm freckling as we made our way down and, for many years, displayed my cedar freckles proudly! Now they are lost amid the marks of old age!

Biblical references to the cedars are interesting. I understand that they are mentioned 75 times. I shall mention only a few:

> "The righteous .... Shall grow like a cedar of Lebanon"
> **Psalm 92:12**

> "The trees of the Lord are watered abundantly.
> The cedars of Lebanon which He has planted
> Wherein the birds make their nests."
> **Psalm 104:16, 17**

> Pharaoh of Egypt likened to the cedar –
> "Behold I will liken you to a cedar in Lebanon

with fair branches and forest shade
and of great height
its top among the clouds"

Ezekiel, 31. (A poem, an extended
metaphor – well worth reading)

"The sycamores have been cut down,
but we will put cedars in their place –"
We always think we will build better next time!

Isaiah 9:10

"Wail, O cypress, for the cedar has fallen ...."
Zachariah 11:1-3

"I dwell in a house of cedar,
 but the ark of God dwells in a tent"
David resolves to build God's house – 2 Samuel 7:2

Solomon builds the Temple and his Palace
"The table for the showbread was of cedar
And the porch of pillars in his palace which was called
"The house of the forest of Lebanon."

Senacherab's boast to Hezekiah when
threatening to attack Jerusalem:

"I have gone up the heights of the mountains
to the far recesses of Lebanon
I felled its tallest cedars
Its choicest cypresses
I entered its farthest retreat
Its densest forest."

2 Kings 19 v. 23

Cedarwood is strong, but easy to work. Its resin is fragrant and so it has its natural insect repellent: it is therefore long lasting. The roots stretch out as far as its branches, giving the tree great stability. It is very slow growing. Gertrude Bell took home some cones and from their seeds a tree at her home, Rousham, and one in a friend's garden at Wallingford in this century have reached maturity. The cedar is one of my favourite trees. I am glad there are many to be seen in public parks and gardens. Its blue-green colour is unique.

I believe it was on this holiday that I was travelling in a hired car, with a silent driver (very little language between us) when he suddenly uttered the word 'Palmyra' and, taking a hand from the wheel, pointed right. "Palmyra" I said, and caught a hazy glimpse of Zenobia's great city. I gave it a friendly wave and almost said, "See you sometime." Of course, it had become in that instant my third great 'near miss'. Petra was the first and Gerash, you remember, was the second. With the all-before-me confidence of youth, I always thought I would return.

Cedars under snow

If I had missed Palmyra, I carried with me forever clear impressions of Baalbec. Gertrude Bell, on returning there (lucky lady!), wrote: "I had almost forgotten how beautiful this place is. Except Athens, there is no temple group to touch it!" I console myself that I have walked around the Acropolis several times, once by moonlight, with a few friends, all of us in evening dress. There is something romantic and unforgettable about that! A night of unmatched beauty. No tourist crowds, just us: a perfect scene, a perfect sky, a night never to forget. But I have wandered back to Europe. I must return to the Middle East.

The Road to Bethlehem

From Jerusalem, Bethlehem is between 3½ and 5½ miles; some say one, some say the other! It must be a country road!

Occasionally, I went to Bethlehem by bus, sometimes I was taken by car, but it was far more rewarding to walk. Choose a day when it is not too hot. It may not be as enjoyable now as it used to be; even then one could wish there was not so much traffic; now the traffic may be much worse. Early morning is a good time to set out usually. You may be able to feel you are on a country road; there are some glorious views. There are also one or two interesting stopping places. The most interesting thought, however, is of the people who have walked this way in the past: the Israelites and Philistines whose descendants, the new Israelites and Arabs, still walk here most often.

Bethlehem – Flowers in Foreground

Then came Egyptians, Assyrians and Babylonians, each in turn conquerors unquestionable; Romans and Greeks, Roman conquerors again; in their wake, Greeks – our Bible came to us through their languages. Persian and Moslem and Crusading armies marched this way, Saracens and Turks. Then French and German and British came on the scene and certainly walked this road. British and allied soldiers and civilians came in the late 19th and 20th centuries, the British as rulers. All walked the road, even as I walked it in the 1940's. What a lot of ghosts one might meet on the way. What footsteps might have echoed, the tramp of soldiers' boots – all sorts of boots – the soft steps of sandals, the trot of donkeys, the padding of camels and I am sure bare feet have sometimes kicked the stones or squelched when the rains came. And here am I, once more telling you how good it was to walk in Armenian hand-made shoes!

I must get on a little faster. I think the first thing to look out for, if the views are not enough, is a large stone circle with a hole in it, often called the Magi's Well or the Well of the Star. There is an attractive legend that the star that guided the Wise Men disappeared for a while, perhaps obscured by a cloud. They grew thirsty and dispirited and stopped for a drink to quench their thirst. Then they saw their star reflected in the water and could go on their way rejoicing. It is also said that Mary rested here and drank from the water also; so some call it Mary's Well.

Pilate's Aqueduct is the next point of loitering; it is said to have supplied a stone for that well we have just passed. Soon, if you search for them, you may be able to find a few stone water pipes half hidden (Perhaps there now). Pilate wanted to bring water from Solomon's Pools to Jerusalem. There was not enough money available (a modern predicament!). Pilate solved it by taking money from the rich Treasury of the Temple. He made a great mistake and violent protests and suppression resulted. I do not think Pilate was essentially bad – he made mistakes; he had yet to make his greatest mistake.

A little off the road, on rising ground, stands the Greek Orthodox Monastery of Mar Elias. This is sometimes associated with Elijah, but the name may only come from a Bishop Elias, who caused the monastery to be built. I often wonder if this was the monastery where I spent a few nights when we were awaiting our Egyptian evacuees (more of this later). Being a seminary for Greek Orthodox ordinands, they might well have been on vacation when a building was needed for our purpose. I have a vague recollection of the place. It looks impressive from the road. On second thoughts, I believe 'our' monastery was nearer Bethlehem.

The Monastery of Mar Elias

Now it is getting hotter and we need a rest. Quite near is Holman Hunt's seat, a stone seat that faces towards the hills of Moab. The view from here inspired Holman Hunt, especially perhaps, to paint "The Scapegoat", a painting which, seen in reproduction in childhood, moved one to a sympathy with goats; little lambs always had my affection and I am glad I once had a pet one of my own. (A clergyman once referred to sheep as senseless: I would have none of it. How could he? Christ the good Shepherd, Christ the Lamb. I suppose I was lucky enough to have farming ancestry and he was not. I would claim to have sense and sensibility towards animals; neither sentimentality nor scorn).

"Let him go for a scapegoat into the wilderness"

Back to Holman Hunt. His other famous painting was "The Light of the World". (I have a prayer book with a reproduction of this in silver which I believe was a Confirmation gift to my mother). Holman Hunt had been about to give up painting when suddenly this painting made him famous: thereafter, he went to live and paint in the Holy Land. The seat many people rested on (I hope it is still there) was erected by his widow. It has been said to have one of the finest views in the world – Jerusalem and Bethlehem can both be seen at this point and the countryside in all directions.

A rubbing of the silver cover of my mother's Prayer Book. The Light of the World was a popular painting up to the 1939-45 War

Rachel's Tomb

Our last stopping place is Rachel's Tomb, significant for Jews, Moslems and Christians. It is near a fork in the road where you can take either the road to Hebron or the road to Bethlehem. Jews and Moslems may choose Hebron, where Abraham was buried; Christians are more likely to continue on the road to Bethlehem.

Before going into Bethlehem, we might visit the Shepherd's fields, green or golden, according to the time of year. Snow covered, sometimes, at Christmas.

Rachel's tomb

Dressing Up

Bethlehem is a small town, mostly Christian. I had an Arab colleague whom I visited there (Miss Sifri) and enjoyed many a scrumptious tea in her house, remembering of course, to eat much, as I liked my hostess. I also remember visiting the home of one of the girls I taught. She was a very sweet girl, rather shy, always happy and smiling. Her mother was just the same and most hospitable. I am sorry I cannot remember their names.

It was my great privilege there to try on the mother's wedding dress, a very superior version of the garments one saw worn for doing quite ordinary things in the homes and streets of the little peaceful town, for such it then was. One can see women working on their rich embroidery.

The outfit I was allowed to try on had a beautiful gold-embroidered velvet jacket. I wish I had brought home one like it. It would have been a friend for life. I brought home things of much less value, a few pieces of mother of pearl work, an olive wood covered Bible, olive wood napkin rings and star of Bethlehem lace table mats.

Me; Bethlehem in the background

The Velvet Jacket

Bethlehem

Bethlehem is the City of David, the home of Boaz and Ruth, the great-grandmother of David, the birthplace of Jesus. Beit Lahm – the house of bread; Jesus the Bread of Life. "O little town of Bethlehem, how still we see thee lie", so says the Christmas carol. Usually, when I went to Bethlehem, it was a place of quiet and stillness; but not at Christmas time.

Christmas in Bethlehem is a significant memory for many people, even those who have only heard its bells 'over the air', as shared in a recorded service. I was lucky to be able to attend several Christmas services, once in near-summer weather, once in deluging rain and once when it was snowy. If the snow or rain were too heavy, then we did not go: the little car available said 'No, enough is enough!' I have heard it said that Christmas never comes to the Holy Land "in the bleak mid-winter", but I know that it can; not every year, but sometimes. I can remember flasks of hot cocoa being prepared to sustain us for the Christmas adventure.

Christmas in Bethlehem was a busy, almost bustling time during the 1939-45 war years; many soldiers congregated there, either stationed near-by or coming on leave at that time. My husband was one of these men and I am letting him give his account of Christmas in the Holy Land.

Christmas in the Holy Land

There are holiday brochures aplenty with this eye-catching caption. As a soldier of nearly 60 years ago, to be posted away from desert fighting in North Africa was pleasant indeed; to be sent on duty to Jerusalem was as near to paradise as war days could offer. All fares and expenses paid: such was my good fortune.

It rains in the Holy Land only during the winter season, which is roughly from late November till mid-February; but there are plenty of short, dry spells at times and Christmas tide was one of them: bright sun by day and bright star-lit skies at night. On such a Christmas Eve did hundreds of us service men make our way from Jerusalem along the winding road to Bethlehem some three and a half miles away, passing Rachel's Tomb clear against the star-lit sky. Some had lifts on trucks, while others walked and enjoyed the exhilarating cool night air.

By 9 p.m., the little town of Bethlehem was packed. Christians of all denominations have their rightful place in the Church of the Nativity, built over the Grotto below the floor and once the Stable to shelter the New Born Jesus. Roman Catholics in their hundreds were gathering for Midnight Mass in their own Church of St. Catherine close by. A hundred or more of us Anglicans had been organised to stay together and assemble just outside the City, in the Fields of the Shepherds. Shepherd boys dressed much as they had been nearly 2,000 years before had set their flocks to rest, and the sheep were as sheep have always looked. We formed a circular group and sat on boulders or tufts of coarse grass. Our leader, an Anglican padre whom we had known at St. George's Cathedral in Jerusalem, led us in praise, prayer and meditation. It was not physically possible to have a service of communion, but we sang "It came upon a midnight clear", "While Shepherds watched their flocks by night", and others known to you all. We praised God and gave thanks for the coming of His Son to this spot and thence to mankind.

It was a glorious and uplifting experience: we were, or could well have been, on the very spot where the shepherds of old beheld the Star and were made wondrously aware of the coming of the Child of Redemption. No musical instrumental lead had we, not even a tuning fork. We had untrained voices and we had never sung together before, but what of that? At least we sang in tune, with gusto but reverence withal. Only vaguely do I remember my companions and only one clearly and by name: he was an Army chaplain, later to become Bishop of Salisbury and gone to his rest some years ago now.

Our gathering was over. As we made our way back to the Jerusalem road, we heard the singing of Mass from the Catholic concourse. Midnight past, we headed back to the Holy City, twinkling with lights in the distance. Starlight was sufficient to show our way back to billets and bed: the first hour of a Christmas morning, wonderful to enjoy and never to be forgotten.

F.R. Gidney

My own experience of Christmas services was a little different. Only once did I go to the Shepherds' Fields, but always we made for Manger Square and looked up at the high fortress walls, forbidding looking as one thought of a tiny baby and a gentle mother.

Baby in swaddling clothes

Mary bathing the baby (Yugoslavia)

Then we entered the Church by its humbling little doorway by which everyone must enter: no ceremonial entrance for any of the attending dignitaries, for long ago the door was cut down to size to prevent enemies on horseback from entering – or so it is said. Some call it the Door of Humility, for everyone of modern height must bow to enter.

The Church of the Nativity

Inside, the church is large and impressive. It was built in the 6th century by Justinian to replace Constantine's church of the 4th century which was destroyed. The Crusaders did some restoration work and alterations (including the doorway) in the 11th or 12th centuries. It is possible to see mosaics of Constantine's church, where the floor has been opened up to reveal them several feet lower. The nave is dimly-lit, vast and calm and a place of dignity, with 40 reddish-coloured marble pillars, with Corinthian capitals, originally gilded, supporting the roof. There are discernible decorations on some of the pillars and on the walls. St. George is there, and Canute and Baldwin, the first King of Jerusalem.

At the end of the nave, there is an iconostasis belonging to the Greek church; the Armenians have altars to the Virgin and Three Kings; it has been said that the church escaped destruction by the Moslems because, on looking in, they saw the three kings with whom they could identify their own people.

The Grotto of the Nativity is reached by stairs below this part of the church. It is dark, in spite of a number of gold and silver lamps. There is a little chapel with altars masking the manger and the place where the Three Kings knelt. The rock face of the 'cave' is blackened from the smoke of candles lit through the ages, but patterned fire-proof curtains, incense-scented, partly cover the walls. The centre-piece in the grotto is a large silver star set in the floor with an inscription in Latin *"Hic de Virgine Maria Jesus Christus natus est'.*

Always, my friends and I knelt at this spot and prayed.

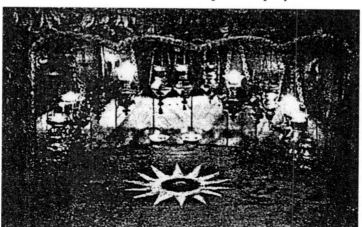

The silver star set in the floor of the Grotto

It was a place where one wanted to pray, but one could not stay for long for there were always others waiting their turn. I remember clearly waiting a long time for a lady, wearing a fur coat, to rise from her knees. The fur coat memory bears out what I have said about wintry weather.

From the Grotto, we moved into the Latin Church of St. Catherine, where their Midnight Mass was about to take place.

By now, you will realise how much pleasure I gain from reading about other people's experience in the Middle East, not least of my friends in print being Sir Ronald Storrs. I will paraphrase and quote from his account of a Christmas Mass that he attended:

"At 10.30, B--- and I drove in a torrent to Bethlehem, which we reached about 11, passing straight into the Latin Church, round and beyond the Orthodox and Armenian. The building was a sharp disappointment: a commonplace eighteenth century vaulted basilica, the walls distempered duck's egg blue, the organ in the place of the East window and the altar and reredos gaudily and tawdrily adorned with tin and tinsel roses and images. On the right front of the nave stood a richly gilt throne with a 'prie-dieu' in front and in the aisle behind, the women, the married ones, in most decorative high mediaeval coifs".

A Bethlehem woman. The veil is said to date back to the Crusaders, whose womenfolk wore such veils.

In the first row of the other side, armchairs (for important guests, including Storrs himself).

"The service had been going on for hours ---- and we had forty-five minutes more before, at midnight, all the bells rang; a deputation of prelates and dignitaries walked down the church, preceded by two cavasses with great staves of office. (There was censing and bowing). The Abbot, a gigantic man with a figure like an apse and considerable carriage, knew apparently but little of his part, and the voice of prayer was frequently merged in the hoarse cue of a very able prompter. The ritual seemed best performed by eight little scarlet-robed Syrian acolytes, ----. At about 1.30 a.m., an immense candle, two inches thick, was lit and presented to the chief guest; others receiving smaller candles. The clergy and guests then led a procession round the church, up the beautiful Greek basilica, through a narrow door and down steep steps into the Crypt of the Manger, the walls and ceiling of which were hung with heavy satin brocade. After a number of prayers and a really impressive hymn, a doll-baby which had been carried round in a little gilt bed was lowered into the recessed niche of the Manger; and the procession, of glittering vestments, rich armorial capes, uniforms and waning candles, paced back the same way, each step accentuated by the two cavasses striking the iron ferrules of their heavy staves against

the stone flagging, with curiously arresting effect. The service contin-
ued till about 2.30 a.m."

The services each year were not unlike this, but not quite so many dignitaries. I also had the pleasure and privilege of attending richly ceremonial
Christmases, Orthodox and Armenian, which take place early in January,
the Eastern churches following the old calendar, the Julian.

Similar ceremonial services we witnessed and I expect something very
much the same can be witnessed today.

In the Bethlehem Bell Tower

Another view of Bethlehem

Evacuees from Egypt

Early in 1942, Rommel appeared to be gaining the upper hand in North Africa and Palestine felt obliged to take a number of evacuees/refugees from Egypt. A large group arrived in Jerusalem in July, just as our summer holidays began. The Government asked for some of our staff to volunteer to run a hostel for them. Peggy Craig and I were assigned to a disused monastery in a remote spot off the Bethlehem Road.

Mar Saba – A Monastery near Bethlehem

We were just beginning to get things organised there, when we were moved to a more modern building on the Bethlehem Road. We were sorry for the group of people introduced to us, uprooted from their homes and thrown together in confined quarters where living was reduced to its simplicities. They were mostly middle aged; we imagined them to be business or professional folk. Most of them were of European extraction, some speaking several languages, and varying in their acceptance of their present circumstances. Peggy and I wondered why these particular people had been evacuated. We almost decided that they must have had something to do with spying for Britain and therefore their lives would be most in danger if they came under German domination.

Moses found that his band of refugees from Egypt became awkward and fractious, although he was seeking to lead them into safety. Our group soon showed signs of refugee discontent, refugee syndrome or complex, or whatever one might call it, to make it easier to deal with. There was an Italian doctor among our group who began by offering his services, but one day surprised us when he did not like the food (perhaps mejedera, Esau's mess of pottage, instead of a good pasta dish.) Suddenly, we heard a crash: he had thrown his entire helping on the floor.

I remember one Greek lady who was always being sorry for me. "You are too young to be doing this: you should be going out with those nice officers. One of them should marry you." etc. – all of which I found rather embarrassing. My answer was a smile and something like "Let's get this war over first."

Various important people visited us to see that things were going according to plan or just to be nice. First there was a Government official, then Lady McMichael the Governor's wife, who had something of a reputation for economical housekeeping: she came to collect swill for her pigs, incidentally, of course. Thereby hangs a tale. As well as British troops coming to Jerusalem, there were increasing numbers of Australians and Americans. All needed to be well fed and enjoyed substantial breakfasts; that meant much more bacon was needed. Neither Jewish nor Moslem food laws allowed them to eat bacon, but both found they could rear pigs and if they could not quite make fortunes, they could make considerable financial gains from the increased demand for bacon. It was said that Jews were selling their grand pianos to buy pigs and Arabs were sacrificing dowries and jewels with the same purpose. We began to talk of the pig boom and then of the pig bubble. Although the Governor's lady had also become devoted to pigs, the Government eventually brought in legislation to prick the bubble. We in Haifa found for a while that, if we wanted meat we could only get pork. Pork and orange sauce sound delicious, but eventually we found it boring.

Our most exalted visitors at our 'camp' were members of the Greek royal family, who were themselves more or less refugees in Palestine. One princess came often to make sure that Greeks were being well treated. She asked more questions than any other visitors.

A Biblical Cavalcade

I was very glad that we had moved to the Bethlehem Road, chiefly because, shortly after dawn, in the incomparable silence and tranquillity of the hour, I could look out of my bedroom window and see a Biblical cavalcade making its way towards Jerusalem. A string of camels, donkeys, an occasional man and a number of women were walking the good three miles to the market near Jaffa Gate. The donkeys were laden with produce, perhaps one carried a woman, but most of the women were themselves laden, bearing on flat trays on their heads tomatoes, cucumbers, courgettes (cusa), eggplants (bringel), lemons, oranges, beans and lettuces. Such processions had been walking that road from time immemorial.

On the way to early morning market. An early impression. Taken from my window!

Of the arrival of such cavalcades, George Adam Smith, writing from Glasgow in 1907, gives the best description I know:

"The cocks crew ... The sky had grown blue in the lower east and above that from purple to pink. Swifts began to fly past the houses: thronging at last till the air was thick with them. A bugle rang out from the citadel ... In the hollow between Scopus and the Mount of Olives, the sky grew red. Two camels entered the Jaffa Gate laden with lemons and knelt groaning on the pavement: the netting burst and the lemons spilt into the shadow. A fruit seller set out his wares on a basket. A black woman, some porters and a few sleepy soldiers crossed the open space inside the gate. In the eastern sky, the crimson had spread to pink, which was followed by a deep yellow, and the first beams of the sun broke across Olivet. The Latin clock struck five. A detachment of soldiers were threading their way...

The lower city, the sanctuary and its court, caught the sunshine and life grew busy. Lines of camels laden with charcoal stalked through the gate: followed by donkeys with wood for fuel. A man swept the street and a boy put the refuse in a bag on a donkey's back. The barber and the knife-grinder took up their posts on the pavement. A small flock of sheep, peasants with eggs and cucumbers and, since it was a summer of more than usual drought, a line of water-carriers from Ain Karim, entered together in a small crowd. There was a shuffling of many feet on the pavements and in the bazaars the merchants were opening their booths."

That description was written about 1907; with very little difference, it could have been written in the early 1940s. Adam Smith concludes:

"And so, through all the centuries, the dawn has broken in Jerusalem, and the hewers of wood and the drawers of water, the peasants

with their vegetables, the sheep for the Temple sacrifices, and all the common currents of the city's life have passed with the sunrise through the gates and stirred the gloom of the narrow lanes with the business of another day."

Arrived at Jerusalem. Morning market impression

George Adam Smith was a Professor at Glasgow University. I had the good fortune some years ago to spot his "Jerusalem" in a library book sale; for a few pence, it has been 'wealth' to me with its wealth of understanding and descriptions of the Holy city.

13. Out and About in Jerusalem

Walk about Zion and go round about her;
Number her towers; mark well her ramparts;
Go through her citadels; corridor her palaces;
Set up her houses – that you may tell them that come af-
*   ter.*

Psalm 48:12 & 13 (Adapted from several translations)

Let us go now for some walks about Jerusalem. Early on, I told you how I was soon taken to the Souk, in the Old City, by a colleague. Not long afterwards, another colleague, the Jewish Hebrew mistress, asked me if I would like to join a group she was taking to the Old City on the next Saturday. I was quite flattered to be the 'new one' who was asked. I did, however, realise later that there was a latent subsidiary – I will not say ulterior – motive in inviting me. Saturday being the Sabbath, the party could not go on buses or exchange money in any way, but this rule could be kept to the letter if I paid and then was reimbursed on Monday. Perhaps I was given a purseful of coins on Friday before sundown. I cannot remember, but I know it was I who had to hand over every sum that the outing required!

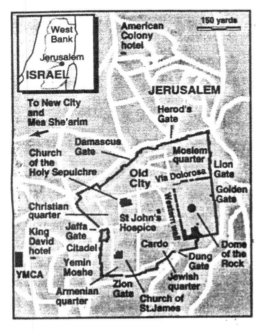

Normally, in those days, there was no problem in walking about Jerusalem. I will begin by taking you round the walls of Jerusalem.

The walls standing now were built by Suleiman the Magnificent about 1540. They are impressive, built of that mellow honey-coloured stone that ensures that we all see Jerusalem the Golden. There are eight gates in the city walls. Their names are fascinating. I usually entered the Old City by the Jaffa Gate, the one most used, sometimes called the Pilgrim Gate or the Gate of the Friend.

If we walk all round the walls, beginning from this gate and turning left (eastwards), the next gate reached is New Gate, then comes Damascus Gate, another principal entry. Herod's Gate comes next, then St. Stephen's Gate, the entrance to the Via Dolorosa. This is the Lion Gate to the Jews. Now we are looking across to the Mount of Olives and then, facing Gethsemane, is the Golden Gate blocked by Saladin and not to be opened till the Messiah comes or, as the Christians say, until Christ's Second Coming.

Orange seller at the Damascus Gate   *The Golden Gate*

Continuing (round the corner) we soon come to the Dung Gate and lastly to the Zion Gate. Then back to the Jaffa Gate.

There were at least three walls and many alterations, additions, renovations, changing the exact course of the walls through the centuries. Solomon, Nehemiah, Hezekiah, Herod the Great, Hadrian, the Empress Eudocia, wife of Theodosius II, c. 450 A.D., all did some building. At different times, there were gates with different names and there have been alternative names to the gates which still exist, e.g. the Gai or Valley Gate, the Fountain Gate, the Gate Genoth (meaning Garden Gate or Gate of Protection), the Sheep Gate, the Fish Gate, the Gate at the Corner, El Bab Sitt Mariam, meaning the Gate of Our Lady Mary (possibly an earlier name for St. Stephen's Gate.) Another gate translates as the Gate of the Old. Enough of walls and gates. What lies within them?

Within the city walls, there are four main areas accorded, or according to, the four main groups of people in the country – the Armenians (Christians), another Christian area, a Jewish area and a Moslem area. As you wander through East Jerusalem, you will find some dwellings in these areas, but dwellings do not dominate. Biblical sites dominate the scene: the Temple Area, whereon stands the now gold domed mosque 'The Dome of the Rock' and 'The El Aksa Mosque'. Nearby is the one remaining temple wall, popularly known as the Wailing Wall, but to the Jews it is the Western Wall. There are many churches, the most important being the Holy Sepulchre, the culmination of the Via Dolorosa (Way of the Cross) which goes along several streets.

It is streets I want to think about next and, as we go, we will come upon some other important biblical and historical sites and sometimes look inside.

Street and place names always fascinate me, along with the making of names. The Arabs are good at it, even for whole areas. In Gertrude Bell's letters, I read Beit Umm ej Jemal, which means, she tells us, "The House of the Mother of Camels" and her next letter was written from Umm er Rumanin, more attractively "The Mother of Pomegranates", but, she adds, there aren't any! The street names are not quite so illuminating – or unilluminating – as these, but still often fascinating. We have David Street, St. Francis Street, Christian Street, Our Lady's Street, Honour Lane, the Street of the Chain, the Street of Bad Cooking and we also have the Church of Zebedee's Fish Shop and the Cheese-makers' Valley. We also have a Cotton Market, Streets of the Taverns, Coppersmiths and Cobblers and a Spice Market. In Christian Street, besides buying holy souvenirs, we purchase candles and see them being made for the many churches.

When Sir Ronald Storrs became Chief Administrator in 1917, after Allenby's victory over the Turks, he did a lot of tidying up. He decided that the names of the streets "should be proclaimed in blue on green tiles, glittering against the sober texture of her walls like chrysoprase and lapis lazuli." I always liked these tiles bearing the three different scripts of English, Arabic and Hebrew. Here are some of the names of streets, some inside and some outside the city walls. Who would not delight in Water Melon Lane (in a hot country, who would not buy one?), Dancing Dervish Street (a little frightening?), Stork lane (no ante-natal clinics, I fear). Biblical names outside the walls were: Street of the Prophets, Nehemiah Road, Street of the Maecabees, St. Paul's Road. And historical names are often redolent of battles long ago; Coeur de Lion Street, Godfrey de Bouillon Street, Saladin's Road, Allenby Square.

For me, the street that meant most was The Street of the Prophets, because there were two places there where I was made welcome and spent happy hours. You might say that at least two modern-day prophets lived there, Christian prophets.

The first of these good people was the Headmistress of the Swedish School and the second the Principal of the Language School. The Swedish School did not teach Swedish, but taught in English and Arabic to poorer and younger children than ours. The Headmistress, Miss Eckblad, was one of the kindliest and most unassuming people I met in Palestine. There are a few references to her in my letters home:

"I've been spending this weekend at the Swedish School. Miss Eck-blad is most kind; she invited me. I am sleeping very high up and can walk out on to the roof and look all over Jerusalem. To come to bed, I have to climb a little twisty staircase. It's a very pleasant change to stay here. Miss Eckblad says I may come whenever I like; it will be nice to have such a homely place to go to."

I went back to the 'homely place' quite often and when I left Jerusalem, Miss Eckblad gave me a Persian lamp. The shade had to be replaced some years ago, but the lamp now stands near our telephone and I remember that dear Swedish lady nearly every day. There are probably many other British people who remember her – an 'ambassador' for her country if ever there was one. She could talk learnedly, philosophically and religiously but, equally, she entertained to tea, along with her assistant, Esther Sven-sen, any young soldier boy and some not so young. She was 'at home' to them every Sunday afternoon. They enjoyed her home-baked teas, as I enjoyed original Swedish cooking at lunch or dinner. My favourite was rolled lamb with spiced prunes. I wish I had her recipe, but even if I had, I know it would never taste so nice.

Not far from the Swedish School was Thabor, the house that was the home of The Newman School of Missions that was commonly known as the Language School, where I tried to learn Arabic. It was *the* place for learning Arabic under its Director, the Revd. Eric Bishop, who was as eru-dite as anyone I met in the city. After the Mandate, he brought his valuable learning to Glasgow University and taught Arabic there. Eric and his wife were most hospitable. I remember that a colleague and I spent a happy, restful weekend there. Their hospitality was immense. They had an adopt-ed Arab daughter, a baby who had been left on their doorstep, I was told.

Thabor, if still standing, will be 130 years old or more by now. In the middle of the 19th century, Dr Schick, a famous architect and archaeologist, built Thabor to be his own home. Bishop Newman, of the American Meth-odist Episcopal Church, acquired the lease in 1888, intending it for his retirement, but he died before he could live in it. His widow bequeathed the house to the American Methodists and it became a Methodist Biblical Institute. Its use was completely changed during World War 1, when it was used as a Turkish Officers' mess.

From 1920 – 1926, Dr Harte, an American Methodist, lived there while he was planning the very fine YMCA which, incidentally, was a great refuge for military men during World War II. In 1928, after an International Mis-sionary Conference, Thabor became the Newman School of Missions for the training of missionaries of all denominations and a centre for the learning of Arabic, Hebrew, Syriac and wide religious studies.

Government officials learnt their Arabic there; nurses, doctors and many others also. It was commonly known as the Language School, but it went far beyond that. I knew of groups learning to read the Greek Testament there. Men in uniform who were considering becoming ordinards after the war, and any soldiers were given a special reading room with a library to escape from army quarters. Many Padres enjoyed the opportunity of being in Jerusalem during the war. A notable one I met at the "Language School" was the Revd. Leslie Farmer of the Methodist Church, who took many men on expeditions in the Holy Land and wrote a book called "We Saw the Holy City". I am indebted to him for many scholarly facts and information about Thabor itself and some other places. He was learning Arabic when I was, and became proficient. I can remember only a few words!

Gertrude Bell makes a number of remarks on the learning of Arabic; "I thought I should never be able to put two words together. Added to the fact that the language is very difficult, there are at least three sounds almost impossible to the European throats. The worst, I think, is a very much aspirated H. I can only say it by holding down my tongue with one finger, but then you can't carry on a conversation with your finger down your throat, can you?" For one sound, I myself was given advice: "Think you are a camel gargling." Well, my acquaintance with camels was not exactly intimate and I found it difficult to imagine one gargling!

First impressions are always significant. One's first experience of a camel can be traumatic! The gargling, or growling, of a camel remained the first alarming impression of the Holy Land for an old lady who arrived there in 1919. No romantic greeting to the Holy City for her!

Gertrude Bell mentions two other problems. "There are five words for a wall and 36 ways of forming the plural. And the rest is like unto it."

Usually, it was possible to manage quite well with very little Arabic, but one incident which occurred when I was on duty in the Boarding House made me think I should make a serious effort to learn more. One day, a distracted washerwoman rushed at me with many words (not understood) and many gestures which led me to the basement, where the laundry was done. There, I found our second washerwoman in even greater distress and there was something bloodstained on the floor. The woman had had a miscarriage. Suddenly, it dawned on me; that might have been a baby, and I was overwhelmed. I was incapable of dealing with the situation. All I could do was to get the Headmistress to come at once. I never felt so young and unequal to real life – or death! I could never have been a nurse, any more than I could have been an Arabic scholar! I resolved to learn more Arabic, but their phrase books deal more with life in the desert than life in a laundry basement, or even on the upper floor of a girls' boarding house. I also learnt by experience that Arab tenses and English tenses did not entirely match. This raised a moral question. I might say, "Have you given in your homework?" "Yes" the reply would come, but the homework was nowhere to be seen. The "yes" had meant "I will do it now, or it might be Bukra (tomorrow – a favourite word, often preferred), quite permissible in Arabic. One tense often seems to fit past and future – no deception intended – just a problem of communication.

Arabic script is a work of art. I learnt to write my name in Arab calligraphy and was very proud of it. I lost the art long ago – alas! My Arabic signature is not extant.

Taking life as a whole, I wish I had learnt Hebrew. It would have been rewarding to be able to read the Old Testament in the original and it would have brought a Theology degree (instead of a Diploma) within my grasp. I once asked a small group of girls to make their own translation from Hebrew into English. One girl produced a beautifully poetic translation and, in discussion, it was agreed that the English translation (A.V. in those days!) came closer to the spirit of the Hebrew than translations into other European languages. I wish I could have tested this for myself. I remained the silent one in the discussion.

From time to time, I commented on my efforts with Arabic in my letters. Here I was, in a fairly optimistic mood: "I'm beginning to enjoy trying to read bits of Arabic, though the grammar is very complicated and I am sure it will take me years to learn the language at all thoroughly. It will be grand when I can carry on a conversation easily."

For me ever to reach that stage, history would have had to leave me in a peaceful Palestine/Israel situation, continuing a career in our continuing schools. At that time, one colleague about my age had a firm vision of the future, with her succeeding as Head in one school and I in another. The golden ball and the golden strings tend not to run straight; they are deflected by many obstacles; they turn and twist and take a zig-zag course.

I have taken you around the walls of Jerusalem. Let us now go inside them. We peeped inside the Jaffa Gate before. It is a good starting point; still sometimes called the Gate of the Friend. We saw it in the early morning and the fruit and vegetable market was just beginning. Imagine it is now mid-morning and very hot. Soon, we shall be glad that the narrow streets are often vaulted or arched and so we are shaded from the sun at least part of the time. The covered ways are dim, but then we come into the light and air again and, for a time, we are glad to be in the shaft of sunlight and see the blue sky. We must watch our feet a little, for the streets are cobbled or rough and seldom level; they twist and turn surprisingly sometimes, too. We feel we have moved back in time. There are men in their long jelabiahs and swathed kaffiehs on their heads; some, who have been to Mecca, wear "turbans" "bandaged" with white. There are Moslem women enfolded all in black chadars and, occasionally, one with a white yashmak, seeing very little, I imagine. Christian women wear long black dresses, mostly embroidered in red, in designs denoting their home areas. On their heads they have white veils, perhaps with some coins from a dowry; and on top of that head-dress, they will often be carrying a basket full of fruit or something quite surprising. There will be men bent double with boxes or baskets on their backs and there will be donkeys with wide and heavy panniers, bearing burdens of all kinds. Sometimes, we will be pushed or knocked because of the narrowness of the crowded thoroughfare. Occasionally, a camel will be driven by, lofty and lordly as his nature is. One hopes the donkeys and the camels are not driven too hard or spurred on by weapons, because of nerves and over-wrought tempers. Standing in doorways there will be men chewing sunflower seeds or nuts in idleness, as some Westerners chew gum. Men will also be squatting or sitting near their booths drinking, the drinks often poured from goat-skins. They may be smoking pungent cigarettes or nargiles (hubble-bubbles) and playing a form of backgammon. There will be noise, shouts of roving vendors, cries you have never heard before. There will be smells of spices and odours, fetid and unmentionable.

Illustration of the Citadel.

Before we plunge into all this, which you will love or hate, let us go into the Citadel, which is just beside the Jaffa Gate. It is also known as the tower of David. King David may have built a tower here, but this one is mediaeval, possibly built by Crusaders. King Herod had a palace here and soldiers seem to have been stationed at the spot from New Testament times to 1917. A good view of Jerusalem's manifold domes, church towers, minarets, roofs of synagogues and huddled dwellings can be seen from the tower.

In the 1940's, a Folk Museum was erected in the Citadel, showing manifold head-dresses typical of different people and different places and many farm instruments, including ox-goads and winnowing fans.

Two relatively modern historical happenings took place just here. In 1898, the opening in the Jaffa Gate was heightened so that Wilhelm II of Germany could ride triumphantly into the city with his impressive entourage. More modestly, in 1917, Allenby entered on foot and then, at the tower, he proclaimed that, under the new order "Every sacred building, monument, holy spot, shrine, traditional site, endowment, pious bequest, or customary place of prayer, of whatsoever form of the three religions, would be maintained and protected, according to the existing customs and beliefs of those to whose faiths they were sacred."

General Allenby entering Jerusalem, 9th December, 1917

Now into David Street. I borrow a description that cannot be bettered (for your delight). We see; "Small, ill-lighted cubicles where the odours of spices and fish commingle; where groceries and carcasses are fully exposed to dust and rain; where the steady tapping of hammers means the cobblers are fashioning the turned-up slippers of coloured leathers; where lintels and doorposts are draped with figs, grapes and viscera of freshly killed sheep; where the desk of the professional letter-writer is seen side by side with fennel, okra and pomegranate."

I think you may also find somewhere to buy a wig, or some dress material, or perhaps a "pewter" jar or other piece of fascinating metal work. How about a tray or a Turkish style coffee set?

Perhaps you have now seen enough, or spent enough in the shopping area. We will go to a nearby church. You may need somewhere more familiar for a while. We will go to Christ Church which is Anglican Victorian Gothic, not the most beautiful of churches, but one of the most friendly. It has a small hospice of excellent reputation and a school for younger children. It is linked to the Church Mission to the Jews. During the war years, Miss Ruth Clarke was its presiding genius, a redoubtable lady, I think, but a very gentle one. Near the church is the one-time home, an old and dignified Arab house, of the first Anglican Bishop in Jerusalem, Dr Alexander, a convert from Judaism, a man of great courage and faith.

Not far away, are two other churches; the Armenian Cathedral of St. James, but we will not go there till Holy Week. We will go instead to the Syrian Church of St. Mark, a little church in a narrow, winding cobbled lane claiming to be the site of the Upper Room and the Last Supper. It is approached through a Crusader gateway and is surrounded by a courtyard. Its priest is known as bishop (in a Biblical way, he is less exalted than bishops in most other churches). He speaks Arabic and Aramaic, Old Syriac – the language of Jesus' time. His church is one of the monophysite churches, believing that Jesus had one nature, not that of man <u>and</u> god. The Syrians call themselves Assyrian and claim to be descended from that one time great nation. They represent the earliest form of Palestinian Christianity and some of their forms of worship are quite primitive. Men and women sit separately in services. They dip their babies three times in the font when baptised and confirm them at the same time. Their font is covered with silver, they say from beaten coins given by mothers when their babies are baptised. They have many icons, one said to have been painted by St. Luke (that is said of many icons in many places!). They use lamps, candles and the sistra, rattled to represent angels' wings.

Their church is sometimes called Jacobite (nothing to do with Scotland!). It was founded in the 6th century by the Bishop of Edessa, Jacobus Baradeus, who took the view, as did the Armenian and Coptic churches, that Christ did not have two equal natures, human and divine, but one divine nature. Much debate took place on this doctrine in the 4th and 5th centuries, particularly at the councils of Nicea, Ephesus and Chalcedon. It was also the theological cause of the split between Eastern and Western Christianity.

There are two places in what is now Turkey where this church still struggles to preserve itself in monasteries, with monks and nuns, where their chief aim is to teach boys their faith, so that it may be preserved. Mar Gabriel is the home of the leading monastery. They use Aramaic (or Old Syriac) the language that Christ spoke. Bettina Selby, in one of her interesting travel books "Beyond Ararat" describes her visit there, where she met with kindness. The second Jacobite monastery, Deir-el-Jarfaram, she found unwelcoming, so, if you want to explore as she did, seek out Mar Gabriel, but, I warn you, the travelling there is only for the intrepid.

In 1976, their Bishop in Tehran was elected as their new Patriarch to succeed Mar Shimun. Up till then, their Patriarchate had always passed from uncle to nephew. A relative (a sister, I believe) had been educated at our school, had gone to Oxford and then returned to the staff, but I am not quite sure of this. In writing of our Boarding House, I have mentioned a new girl from the Assyrian Church; there is another Assyrian Church, the Nestorian founded by Nestoreic, Bishop of Constantinople in the 5th century. It claims to be the true Assyrian church. The Nestorian Church is not now, however, represented in Jerusalem.

Church of the Nativity.

14. The Temple Area

Where we dwell, there is no Temple for the Lord, the Almighty is the Temple

T.S. Eliot; The Rock

So appreciative was he of the beauty of the Temple Area by moonlight, that he seemed thereafter to grudge every moment away from his easel

Sir Ronald Storrs, writing of Winston Churchill

When I hear, or see, or think "The Temple Area", I am filled with sadness. In the destruction by the Romans in 70 AD of that once glorious building, the Herodian temple, the whole of humanity suffered one of its greatest losses, a gleaming gold and white building. No wonder the Jews mourn forever by its last remaining stones, perhaps dating as far back as the time of Solomon.

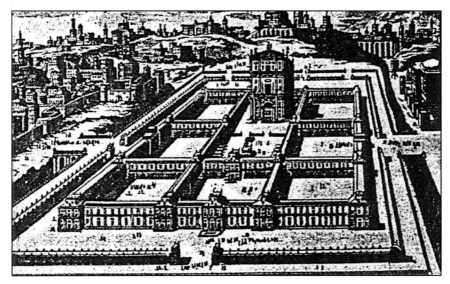

The Temple, as rebuilt by King Herod

I grew up in Canterbury and, almost thoughtlessly, I was absorbed by and absorbed into the Cathedral. Its beauty captured me; its great spiritual symbolism and significance gradually dawned on me. After the 1939-45 war, when I returned home, I realised how lucky I was to see again 'my' cathedral. I could see it more clearly than ever, for so much that had surrounded it had been laid waste by enemy bombs. (How terrible if the cathedral itself had been obliterated). I could half shut my eyes and see it as the mediaeval women of Canterbury of Eliot's "Murder in the Cathedral" must have seen it. How nearly had "Murder in the Cathedral" become "Murder of the Cathedral". I know how Jews must feel at the 'Wailing Wall'. I prefer, with them, to speak of the 'Western Wall'. To 'wail' can be to put grief beyond dignity; to mourn, to lament is the *enduring* grief of grieving – endurance is the keynote of Jewish grieving as they pray in the open, without shelter from sun or rain, without comfort at all, but for that which comes from the Lord.

The Dome of the Rock

How wonderful if we had both the Jewish Temple and the Muslim Mosque, two works of art instead of one, side by side in harmony.

It is not commonly known what Sir Ronald Storrs revealed to me, that when the British took over from the Turks at the end of the 1914-18 war, the Jews began to bring to their Wall chairs and benches for worshippers to rest on. This had been forbidden by the Ottoman Government, but Sir Ronald, the new British Governor, saw no harm in it "on the grounds of reason and humanity". But although the Arabs living in nearby houses had sometimes 'winked at' the introduction of an occasional portable chair being brought in, they now began to fear anything more extensive or permanent, complaining of encroachment on their property and their rights. "Chairs, they feared, would become wooden benches, wooden benches iron benches, iron benches fixed stone benches, with the corollary that covering from above against sun and rain and from the side against cold" would mean new buildings hemming them in. This matter was not settled till 1925, when it came to a head on the Day of Atonement, when benches and chairs were again brought in. When this was reported to Sir Ronald Storrs, he said that those already in could remain for the service, but no more must be added. The Mufti then protested on behalf of the Arabs and the Zionist Commission on behalf of the Jews.

The suggestion was made that the Arabs should erect suitable benches, as the surrounding property was theirs, and for some worshippers at least to be able to sit seemed reasonable – but the seating was never provided and so we see, to this day, standing men and women praying at the Wall. They usually pray separately, just as there is segregation in the synagogues. In a 1998 photograph, I saw a chair and, I believe, in the adjoining cleared area, there are some benches and the sex segregation does not seem to be so marked; there is more open space now and a garden area.

Women at the Western, or Wailing Wall, many years ago

View of the Western, or Wailing Wall –men on the left and women on the right

The story of the origin of the first temple can be found in 2 Samuel 24. David captured the Jebusite city, then came a plague from which the Jews were saved, near the threshing floor of Araunah the Jebusite. David bought the threshing floor and set up an altar there. It was Solomon and not David who actually built on the site the first temple, which lasted till 586 BC.

The second temple was built after the Jews returned from exile in Babylon, where they had been forced to go by Nebuchadnezzar, when he attacked Jerusalem, captured it and destroyed the temple. The second temple was rebuilt from the ruins of the first in 516 BC, under the leadership of Zerubbabel. In the Apocrypha, we can read about Judas Maccabeus who restored the temple, which had been desecrated by the Greek ruler of the area in the second century BC. Antiochus Epiphanes had sacrificed swine in the temple, which caused the Jews under Judas Maccabeus to revolt. Eventually, they were successful and the temple could be restored.

The third temple was an attempt by Herod the Great to gain favour with the Jews. It was begun in 17 BC and was unfinished when Jesus walked the streets of Jerusalem. Titus destroyed the city in AD 70 and burnt down the temple just a few years after its completion.

In AD 135, Hadrian built a temple to Jupiter on the site. The desecration was complete.

In the fourth century AD, in the Byzantine period, Constantine built churches over the Holy Sepulchre and on the Mount of Olives. He did not attempt to replace the temple. Justinian built a church called the Theotokos, the Church of the Mother of God, and some have thought that stood where the Mosque el Aksa now stands. It is even said that the mosque is a conversion of the church. Others say that such a church was on the other side of the city.

In 638, the Moslems conquered the city. Within the Temple Area was the rock of Moriah, from which Abraham was said to have been about to sacrifice Isaac. From this same rock, the Moslems believe Mohammed ascended into the heavens (the rock bears a mark like a footprint). Later, he is said to have returned again to Mecca. The Dome of the Rock was built over this stone by Abd-el-Malik in 687-691. It is sometimes called the Mosque of Omar, but certain authorities say that it is not a mosque and Omar did not build it, he merely cleared the site. Between 705 and 715, the nearby El Aksa Mosque came into being.

From 1099 – 1187, Moslem rule in Jerusalem was interrupted by the Crusaders, who used the buildings in a Christian way, erecting a cross over the Dome instead of a crescent and putting an altar on the rock. The El Aksa became a Templar church. It is said that the order of the Knights Templar was founded here. In London and Cambridge, there are Templar churches, octagonal in shape, like the Dome of the Rock.

When the Moslems took over again, under Saladin in 1187, they restored everything to their own purposes. Jerusalem to them is their third city; Mecca, Mohammed's birthplace, being the first and Medina the second. Originally, Mohammed prayed towards Jerusalem, but Mecca later took precedence. Only Muslims may enter Mecca and Medina. Except for Jews; others may enter the Haram el-Sharif, by the non-Muslim entrance which is in the west wall. It is called bab el-Magharibeh (or Moroccans' Gate). Other gates are the Chain Gate, the most important, the Cotton Merchants' Gate, the iron Gate, the Watchman's Gate and two others, less important.

On entering, I was always struck by the blessing of space. The beauty of the Dome of the Rock, its octagonal shape and perfect proportions are greatly enhanced by the space that encircles it. (I believe that it is a principle of good design to get right the size and shape of spaces surrounding the principal subject. Here, on a large scale, this is perfectly achieved).

It is the gleaming blue tiling that strikes one most forcibly, almost taking one's breath away, on first looking on the Dome. The arcaded walls of the octagon are made of marble, the blue tiling and mosaics and quotations from the Koran encircle it in beautiful Arabic script (installed by Suleiman the Great in the 16th century). No other script is so beautiful. There are several variants in daily use; even the most commonplace is beautiful. They are not easy to learn (I once could write my own name in Arabic but it is an art now quite lost to me).

The interior of the Dome of the Rock

To enter the Dome, one removes one's shoes (and one's arms must be covered). I believe in seemliness for holy places, so have never minded any restrictions. Once inside, one walks on sumptuous carpets. One stands and stares at more beautiful blue tiling. The light is very subdued, largely because the stained glass windows are deeply set in stone framework. To see the windows properly, one must stand directly in front of them. One has to choose whether to approach the Rock first or last. I would let my eye rove first to the two mihrabs, one for Mohammed and one for Jesus, as the guide would always carefully point out. There is also an impressive pulpit for the Imam, made of cedar wood with mother of pearl decorations. A lesser Christian connection is in the grille surrounding the Rock itself. It was erected by the Crusaders and it is said to prevent souvenir hunters chipping off pieces of the rock. Some of the pillars supporting the Dome may have served first in Christian churches. I believe they are all different; some of the capitals are beautifully carved. (One can always enjoy silence in a mosque, not least here in this one of the loveliest places of worship in the world, if not so endearing to me as some village churches at home, or my most loved Canterbury Cathedral). There is a great contrast between mosques and many eastern churches; no human figure must decorate a mosque, while many churches have almost as many – or perhaps more! – human representations on their walls as there are praying figures in the congregation.

Outside, in the sunlight again, we will probably notice the fountain where the Faithful carry out their purifying ablutions before going in to pray. It is correct to wash feet up to the ankle, arms to the elbow and the head to behind the ears. Also, on the Haram, we notice what looks like a miniature of the main building, which some say was a pattern for the Dome itself. There is another tiny cupola which the English should notice, dedicated to St. George, or is it to Elijah, or perhaps to both. In some strange way, the

The Mosque of Al Aqsa,
formerly the Crusader Church

Moslems seem to be able to identify the one with the other. Yet another dome is interesting because it is called the Dome of the Chain. A chain dangles within it and it is a place of justice; if a prisoner tells a lie, a link of the chain is said to fall on him, thus labelling him a criminal.

There are some administrative buildings in a far corner of the Haram, but there are two important buildings left to see; the El Aksa Mosque and Solomon's Stables, which are not far from the gate by which we entered. I have already mentioned that this mosque of the 8th century might have church links. It is an impressive building, with seven aisles and beautiful mosaics on a gold ground beneath its cupola. It was at the entrance to this mosque that King Abdullah of Trans-Jordan was assassinated in 1951, when entering with his grandson Hussein, the succeeding ruler of Jordan.

The Mount of Olives and Gethsemane

The Mount of Olives is scarcely a mountain and Mount Zion and Mount Scopus, close to it, are also no more than hills. The Mount of Olives is approximately 2,700 ft. above sea level, but Jerusalem itself is about 2,500 ft. above sea level. So Olivet is not difficult to climb. It is also not far from the centre of the city – a Sabbath day's journey. What that means has been much discussed. It is said to have been 2,000 Jewish cubits (980 yards), i.e. less than a mile. "As the crow flies" the summit of the Mount of Olives is only about half a mile, but no doubt winding paths would make it more.

It is a glorious sunny morning here as I write, and it is easy to recall Palestine: not too hot yet, a good day to walk to the Mount of Olives, to go up one of the paths that wind quite steeply till we suddenly see the wonderful view all around. Then we will look at the buildings that Jesus never saw, but nearly all of which remind us of Him.

In my velvet-soft Garabedian shoes (not the Orthopaedics I now wear!) I could enjoy the climb through rocky ground and a few cultivated patches within low stone walls, past some olive trees or pines, or fig trees. A rest would be welcome beneath a tree or two as the day grew hotter; but the heat was often tempered by a little gentle breeze as we reached the summit. I have ignored the view of Jerusalem behind me, we will pause for that on the way down. We have reached the summit and there is the distant view, the Judean hills, the barren desert, encircling the ink blue patch of the Dead Sea and then the tawny pinkish purple hills of Moab beyond. A moment to sit on a rock or on a low wall and then we give our attention to the Chapel of the Ascension, now owned by the Moslems, and situated in the Arab village of El-Tua on the road to Bethany (El-Azariya – which some say derives from the name of Lazarus). In the 12th century, the Crusaders built the octagonal chapel and left it open to the sky, as befitting the idea of Christ's Ascension from that point.

Within the little chapel there is a marble slab with an imprint on it, said to be that of Jesus' foot as he ascended to heaven. This idea reminded me of a similar 'footprint' of Mohammed in the Dome of the Rock. The Moslems, acknowledging Jesus as a Prophet, accept His ascension and, quoting the

Koran, say, "They did not kill him, they did not crucify him, they only had his likeness." This fits in with their idea that he went from Gethsemane to the top of the Mount and there ascended. It also fits in with the idea of an obscure Syrian sect that Simon of Cyrene died instead of Jesus. To me, an unlikely idea.

The Chapel of the Ascension.

Now, with my affection for their sister nuns in Ain Karim, I want to visit the nuns in the nearby Monastery of the Ascension. They are very poor; I have noticed before how they dispense cool drinks hospitably in cracked or chipped saucerless cups, but they dispense kindness to warm the heart and now I hope they will let us climb the 214 steps to the top of their land-mark tower and look, not only towards the view we have already seen, but also back towards Jerusalem, gleaming in the sunlight and golden, even though the Dome of the Rock has not yet been lit up by the gold of the wealth of oil, but is leaden blue-grey instead. I am always old-fashioned: I have only seen the gilded dome in photographs, but I sometimes feel the more sombre dome seemed to be taking a more proper place in the picture. It is like something in an old painting, its colour soft and changing with the light.

Another dominant tower on the mount is that of the Augusta Victoria Hospital. Kaiser Wilhelm II and his wife came to Palestine in 1896 for the dedication of the Lutheran Church of the Redeemer, a reconstructed Crusader church. The German community and their friends then raised the money for the 'German Hospital' as a gift on the occasion of their monarchs' Silver Wedding. After the First World War, the building became for a time the Mandate's Government offices. Badly damaged by an earthquake in 1927, the government gave it up and it was eventually restored as a hospital again. A bronze statue of the Kaiser and Kaiserin was erected and mosaic portraits of them adorned the chapel ceiling. I do not know what it is like now.

From German royalty, we move to French. A French princess gave the property where we visit a third church, the Pater Noster Church, which also has a convent – of Carmelite nuns. In the church, the Lord's prayer is inscribed on tile panels. I have heard it said that there are 35, or 44 and even as many as 80 different languages used, some in scripts strange to the Western eye. I was interested in the scripts, but never counted the number. It is said that Jesus first gave the prayer after a visit to Martha and Mary in Bethany.

You can now turn aside and go to Bethany, where there is a 'Tomb of Lazarus'. I don't like looking at tombs. I shall not accompany you here, nor to the Tomb of Mary, near the foot of the Mount. When I was in Jerusalem, I only once visited what was then known as Gordon's Tomb (because he discovered it) and is now known as the Garden Tomb. Gordon's Tomb, of course, is not on the Mount of Olives. There was no garden when I went there. Now, I believe, it is a pleasant beflowered place for rest and prayer. I think the tomb is just a typical one of the time, worth seeing, more acceptable, perhaps, to Protestant Westerners than the marble structure in the Church of the Holy Sepulchre but, as tradition holds, less likely to be authentic. Some of my Scottish friends might be interested to know that, in the garden here, is buried the heart of John Crichton Stuart, Marquis of Bute.

Bethany

I digress. Digression, or diversion, or turning aside on the mountain is almost unavoidable. In my day, there was not only a 1914-18 war cemetery, but also the fine Hadassah Hospital and the Hebrew University of Scopus – inviting 'digressions'. Now the main Jewish Hospital and University buildings have moved elsewhere.

So, on down the hill to Bethphage, where the honoured ass was found for Jesus to ride. You know I like donkeys and I like G K Chesterton's poem:

> "Starve, scourge, deride me: I am dumb.
> I keep my secret still.
> Fools! For I also had my hour;
> One far, fierce hour and sweet:
> There was a shout about my ears,
> And palms before my feet."

How appropriate that the suffering Saviour should choose the derided donkey – who likewise shoulders so many human burdens, albeit the material and physical, rather than the mental and spiritual.

On Palm Sundays, I often joined the Pilgrim Walk following the route that Jesus must have taken on that fateful day.

Very soon now, we come to the best possible view, a nearer one than we had higher up, of the city itself and, somewhere here, Jesus uttered the cry "How often would I have gathered thy children together, even as a hen gathereth her children under her wings." How that endears Jesus to me, more perhaps, than all the sermons I have heard. The comparison is so exactly as I saw it as a child. I could often be found among the hens and their chicks and it was my first joy in counting to number the little fluffy birds who could just manage to 'jump' up onto the handled bowl of food I was holding for them. I wonder if the boy Jesus did much the same. I share his sadness today.

Our route from Bethany was, as I said, the one Jesus took on Palm Sunday and he stopped at about this point and saw the city looking its most beautiful. He loved it and he must leave it. In Chapter 19 of St. Luke's Gospel, we read, "And when he was come near, he beheld the city, and wept over it, saying, if thou hadst known, even thou, at last in this thy day, the things which belong unto thy peace! But now they are hid from thine eyes."

How many ordinary people have wept over Jerusalem since then? At this moment, many prayers go up that she may know, that negotiators may know "the things which belong to her peace." (May 1998)

At the approximate spot where Jesus wept for Jerusalem, there has been built, since I was there, a little church called Dominus Flevit (Jesus Wept). One might feel that there were enough buildings, enough churches on the Mount of Olives already, but I have sympathy with this one and, having seen it only in photographs, I think I might like it, architecturally. I am pleased to see that, behind the altar, there is simply plain glass and the Jerusalem view in the 'reredos'. I first saw this done in New Zealand. Both pictorially and symbolically, I found it a very welcome new idea.

Now we come, a short walk away, to one of my favourite Jerusalem churches, the Russian Orthodox Church of St. Mary Magdalene, on the outskirts of Gethsemane. This was given by Tsar Alexander III, in memory of his mother Marie Alexandrovna. It also contains the tomb of the Grand Duchess Elizabeth, sister of the last Tsarina and wife of the Grand Duke Sergius, who was murdered in 1918. I have already told you, at Ain Karim, how the loyalty and love of the gentle Russian sisters for their Royal Family seemed to follow naturally their love for their Saints and their Lord. The nuns have a favourite picture in this church of Mary Magdalene presenting an egg to Pontius Pilate as she begs for the body of Jesus for burial. Something we often forget is that the Easter Egg is a symbol of Resurrection. The little white church, with its seven mellow golden onion-shaped domes, brings a gentleness to the sadness and harshness of some of the Mount of Olives scene. It is half-hidden in its garden of trees, olives, pines and aspiring cypresses. The cypress is the best tree to represent Christ's Ascension and the ascension of the human spirit. If I had to name my favourite tree, it might well be the cypress, and if I had to choose my favourite church, I think it would be this one, certainly my favourite in the Middle East, rivalled, perhaps, but in a different way, by some village churches in England.

There is yet another church to see: nearer to the foot of the Mount is an impressive twentieth century Latin church, the Church of the Agony, more popularly called the Church of All Nations. It is very near the main road, but on a Maundy Thursday evening, I always found it quite quiet. This church was built about 1925, where Byzantine and Crusader churches had been before, sheltering the Rock of Agony where Jesus prayed that the cup might pass from him. It is a spacious church, cool and dimly lit through alabaster windows. There are many little domes forming the roof and each of these was financed by different nations – hence the Church of All Nations, a welcome name for a church to have.

Now we are at Gethsemane. The name derives from the Hebrew 'Gath-Shamma': oil press. When the Moslems had possession, they called it 'field of flowers'. It is said that olives have been growing on the slopes of the mount for over three thousand years. True or not, story has it that when Noah let out a dove from the Ark to see if the waters were abating, it was an olive leaf that the bird plucked to bring him the good news for which he was waiting. The first Biblical mention of the olive is in 2 Samuel 15-30: "David went up the ascent of the Mount of Olives, weeping as he went." He was weeping because his favourite son, Absalom, had incited rebellion against him.

Olives are now fewer on the Mount than they once were, but they will always grow there. They do well in rough, stony soil. They say the olive tree never dies, but what really happens is the sending up of young shoots, each one of which can become a new tree. These shoots are the 'little olive branches' we refer to in a family. The old gnarled trees – a strange beauty of old age – which we see in Gethsemane, may be hundreds of years old but it is unlikely that they are those which sheltered Jesus; more likely they are *descended* from trees of Jesus' time.

The Church of All Nations (Latin).

I may like the tapering cypress better for its beauty, but the olive must be the native tree for usefulness in the Holy Land. I expect that when I was there I consumed olives or olive oil every day. It has just occurred to me that old people were said to take a small cup of olive oil every day in their pursuit of good health and long life. Many of my former colleagues I know have lived long lives – ninetieth birthday cards have flown about (I have one to write today, and soon one for a non-Palestinian colleague who was 'eccentric', it was thought in England, for taking daily spoonfuls of olive oil! – so buy it!). Olive oil was also used for cooking, for lighting and for washing. It was used for solemn anointing, for welcoming, for curing wounds, or even snake bites. Olives can be eaten in a homely sandwich or at fashionable cocktail parties, elegantly on sticks.

Ancient oil presses can be found in many places (I saw them on the Mount and in Ain Karim – usually half hidden). Today, the pressing is done in a mechanical centre. Children have holidays from school, or they

Picking Olives.

did, to help out at harvest time, about the end of September. They probably enjoy climbing the trees to get the last olives down, those that resisted the shaking of the trees or the beating with sticks. There must not be too much roughness because only unblemished ones will keep. The women carefully prepare them for storage in tins, while enjoying a gossip.

In the Franciscan part of Gethsemane, you will see the oldest olive trees, centuries old; one or more propped up by stone or cement. There, near their church, you will also see a pretty garden. But move to the Russian part of Gethsemane and you may find it more peaceful and, perhaps, more like the place where Jesus and his disciples went from time to time to rest and pray. That last fatal night was all the more sad for its dreadful events having been enacted in a favourite place of peace.

I do not think that one can visit Gethsemane as freely now.

Gethsemane : Old Olive Trees and St. Mary's Church behind.

Via Dolorosa

When we were looking at the walls of Jerusalem and then pausing at the gates, I said that if we enter at St. Stephen's Gate (known as the Lion Gate to the Jews), we shall soon find ourselves walking along the Via Dolorosa, taking approximately the Way of the Cross. The route has been altered over time and it is not at the same level as it was when Jesus carried his cross that way. It is a way of pilgrimage and what we think of as we walk is probably what really makes the pilgrimage. I used to like walking that way and seeing ordinary people, especially the dwellers of the Old City, going about their daily occasions past the Stations of the Cross and under the mediaeval arches.

Jesus in life and on the way to his death, walked where ordinary people walked and looked upon them doing ordinary things. Some would take notice of Him, some would not. Other condemned prisoners would have walked that way too.

Enter St. Stephen's Gate and almost at once you see, to the left, the Church of St. Anne, perhaps marking the spot where Mary was born: her parents, Anne and Joachim, lived there. Within the Church Area is the Pool of Bethesda, where Jesus healed the rather ungrateful paralytic. There are always the grateful and the ungrateful. It was not till 1294 that the most probable final walk of Jesus was mapped out by one who was grateful and wanted to follow this way. Ricoldus of Monte Croce went to Jerusalem "in order that the memory of Christ's sufferings might impress itself deeper in the mind and that the blood of Christ, shed for our salvation", as he said, "might become unto me strength and support, to enable me to preach and die for Him who, by His death, gave life to me." The Via Dolorosa has been walked ever since.

We are in the Old Muslim quarter of the city and pass the Gate of the Tribes leading into the Temple Mount on our left. Protecting the Temple Area was the Antonia Fortress, covering a larger area than now and embracing or linked with Herod's Palace and the seat of the Roman Governor, the Praetorium. It is most likely that this spot is where Jesus was condemned, on a raised pavement or stone, Gabatha to the Jews (Lethostrobas to the Greeks). – St. Matthew 27:22-26.

The Franciscan Convent of the Flagellation and the robing in purple and crowning with thorns is only a few yards from the Antonia tower and the Sisters of Zion Convent of Ecce Homo is adjoining it. These convents are at the first and second stations of the cross.

To reach the Church of the Sisters of Zion, we descend a number of stone steps. One is greeted by a little man who clangs a great bell to summon Mother Mary, who speaks English with a charming French accent. She is devoted to her work, her church and her Saviour. She exudes joy and faith. There are candles to lighten the gloom of this underground shrine, but it is really lit by Mother Mary's radiance. We can bear the thought that it was here that Jesus took up his Cross.

Ecce Homo – Altar of the Basilica

The Ecce Homo Arch begins outside in the street but continues within the church. It dates from Hadrian's time. It commemorates the moment when Pilate addressed the crowd and said "Behold the Man" and was founded by a Jewish convert, Father Ratisbone. He also provided for a Girls' School and Orphanage still run by the French Sisters. All this happened as late as 1842, so it was about 100 years old when I visited it. Mother Mary led us down some more steps to a pavement, a Roman road marked to prevent horses slipping and with gutters at the sides. We were also shown lines for a gambling game scratched into the stone, said to be the signs of the soldiers, who whiled away the time while guarding their most patient prisoner. Something Mother Mary deeply treasured was a replica of the Shroud of Turin, the face of Jesus imprinted on linen. Mary looked on that face with deep devotion. Even those without belief in its authenticity gained something from looking on it with her and sharing her sincere devotion.

Since 1947, there has been a small chapel built by Poles to mark the third Station of the Cross, the place where Jesus fell for the first time. Above the door there is a sculptured stone of Jesus falling under the heavy burden he is forced to carry.

The fourth Station is marked by a small 'Chapel of the Swooning Virgin' and the Armenian Catholic 'Church of the Virgin Mary's Sorrows' built in 1881. This commemorates the meeting of Jesus with his mother, a tradition not authenticated in the gospels. He must surely have thought of her at this time.

The fifth Station is the spot where Simon of Cyrene came to Jesus' aid. St. John says he helped Jesus with the Cross, the other gospel writers say that he carried it for Him the rest of the way. There is a Franciscan chapel at this site (1881). Who was Simon? This is one of the interesting questions of the Bible. He was one of those characters who have only a 'walk on' part – that surely is the part of most of us in life – with which we should be content, just being useful when occasion arises.

Cyrene was an important town in Cyrenaica on the coast of North Africa (Libya now). It had been under Roman rule since 96 BC. Who was Simon? He could have been a Roman back in Jerusalem on business, he could have been a Cypriot Jew, for it has been claimed, especially in Cyprus, that he came from Kyrenia, not far from Cyrenaica. Simon is a Jewish name and so he was most probably a Jew. Was he a farmer? He came in from his fields, from the country. Cyrenaica was a fertile district. Or he could have had land in Palestine. Was he a convert already, or did he become one after carrying the Cross? St. Mark says that he was the father of Alexander and Rufus, known to the early Christian community. We shall never quite know who he was, but only what he did on one day.

The sixth Station. There is a 'House of Veronica' here. The house is only about 300 years old, but its cellar is the crypt of an early church. There is a Melkite chapel run by Little Sisters of Jesus. Veronica wiped Jesus' face with her handkerchief (Sudarium) which had an imprint of this face on it thereafter. Was the woman Berenike or does her name come from 'vera ikon' (true image). Such pictures on linen were called 'veronicae'.

Seventh Station. A Franciscan chapel (1875) commemorates the second fall of Jesus under the weight of the Cross.

Eighth Station. There is a stone here marked with a cross and the inscription ICXC NIKA – 'Jesus is victorious'. Here Jesus told the waiting women to weep not for Him but for themselves and their children – Luke 23: 28-30.

Ninth Station. A pillar marks the place where Jesus fell the third time. It is above some steps leading to the roof of the Holy Sepulchre and a Coptic Church.

The remaining Stations are inside the Church of the Holy Sepulchre.

- Station Ten. The robe is taken off Jesus.
- Station Eleven. Jesus is mounted on the Cross.
- Station 12. Jesus dies. Golgotha Calvary = brain case, skull. Above Greek Chapel of Adem (Adam's skull found there). Jesus died at the place of the skull.
- Station 13. The body of Jesus is laid on a stone slab, the Stone of Unction, the anointing of the body.
- Station 14. Jesus is buried and from this spot takes place the Resurrection.

Long tradition has held these places sacred. It is not easy to establish with certainty their total authenticity but it is good to walk the Via Dolorosa early in the quiet of the morning or with a pilgrim group threading through the busy city, for there were crowds around Jesus. We must be touched by the compassion of such ordinary, unknown people as Simon of Cyrene and Veronica. Some find the Holy Sepulchre too overlaid and ornate but it has long been a place of genuine devotion.

Station 13, The Stone of the Anointing, Church of the Holy Sepulchre, Jerusalem.

15. Jerusalem at Easter

25th April, 1943

Above the streets, the muezzin calls
From minaret to minaret
Lest, busy with the day's concern
The Prophet's law his sons forget
Another walked these crowded ways
Who laid no law upon his own
That they should turn at priestly cry
And daily thus their faith make known
But his the high and gallant way
Adventure's path to victory
"Stand forth! And dare the way of love;
By this, men know ye follow me."

by Kathleen Hatton

Holy Week in Jerusalem

The greatest drama in history took place during Holy Week, and in Jerusalem drama and religion are one, particularly in the ceremonies of the Orthodox Churches. They mingle oriental symbolism with the simplicity of our mediaeval religious drama, teaching through action and colourful scene.

Since the Eastern Churches follow the old Julian calendar, and not the Gregorian, there are often two Easters in Jerusalem. This is fortunate for the Westerner, for he can then attend his own services and some of the many of the other churches. It is impossible to attend them all in one year.

During the last week of Our Lord's life, Jerusalem was crowded and tense; so it always is in modern times. Passover comes just before Easter and the Muslim Nebi Musa more or less coincides. In the more peaceful times that I remember, pilgrims crowded into the city and swarmed through the streets, the narrow streets of the Old City. Romans, Turks, British, Israelis have all in their turn drafted in extra guards to keep the peace. Even within the Church of the Holy Sepulchre itself, quarrels are liable to break out, for this is a church shared by Catholics and most Eastern churches. The Custodian of this ancient church is a Moslem, which may seem strange, but at least he is neutral. The Anglican Bishop has been known often to come to the rescue and arbitrate when someone has allowed his broom to sweep the wrong patch of floor, or some other line of demarcation has been infringed.

Holy Week in Jerusalem begins on the day before Palm Sunday, known as Lazarus Saturday. In the Church of the Holy Sepulchre (built over the traditional sites of Golgotha, and the tomb of Christ) a series of processions, representing the different churches, circles the Stone of Unction, where it is said Jesus' body was anointed for burial. The clergy wear many coloured vestments and red-cassocked choir boys carry silver-coloured books, banners, censors, holy water vessels and crosses flashing blood-red rubies, emeralds, amethysts and crystals. Lit up by candles the dim (often heavily scaffolded) church takes on a magical quality.

The Church of the Holy Sepulchre.

On Palm Sunday, many of the churches, including Anglicans, organise walks from Bethany to Jerusalem, retracing the route by which Jesus came over the Mount of Olives from the home of Martha and Mary. In their quietness, these contrast with many of the other events of Holy Week. There seems nothing incongruous about reading the Bible passages that are relevant while a stray donkey or a sheep or a goat crosses the rugged and dusty path. The way lies through the old olives of Gethsemane and past the place where Jesus wept over Jerusalem. The city is gleaming and golden across the Kedron Valley. We see where Jesus is said to have entered in as they cried ' Hosanna'. The spot is now marked by a blocked arch, known as the Golden Gate. The Jews say the gate will re-open when the Messiah comes and the Christians say that it will open again at Christ's Second Coming.

Two services of note are held on Palm Sunday, one in the Armenian Cathedral called 'The Ceremony of the (Second) coming of Christ' and the other, a much humbler observance in the Syrian Church of St. Mark called ' The Bridegroom's Coming'. The Armenians are artistic people and their cathedral is beautiful, decorated with tiles of their making and lit with hundreds of little lamps filled with olive oil. As we enter on Palm Sunday, the church is dim, the sacred pictures are veiled and a curtain screens the altar. The clergy are vested in blue and red and purple, richly embroidered in gold and silver. Outside the curtain, the Patriarch begins to intone: "Open unto us, O Lord, open unto us the door of pity; to us who call upon Thee with weeping." A voice replies from within. Eventually, as the congregation joins in with an imploring "Open unto us", the curtain is drawn aside to reveal an altar blazing with lights; children unveil the paintings and the singing rises to a ringing ululation. So the joy of being admitted to heaven is symbolised.

The Syrians, who still use a language close to Aramaic, are few and poor. Their service lacks the richness and joy of the Armenians.

Maundy Thursday begins the real crescendo of ceremonies. 'Maundy' is a corruption of 'mandate' – the mandate the disciples received to love one another. Some of the Orthodox churches have re-enactments of the Lord's act of love and humility in washing the feet of His disciples.

The Greek Orthodox Church erects a simple platform in a convent courtyard to represent the Upper Room; they hang a holy picture and an olive branch over a wall to represent Gethsemane. Two forms with twelve cushions on them are placed facing each other with a 'throne' at the head. Between the forms a silver ewer and a basin are placed. Choir boys and priests enter wearing blue and black. Some carry candles tied with blue ribbon, three to represent the Trinity, two to represent the twofold nature of Christ. The white bearded, golden crowned Patriarch arrives. A Gospeller intones the feet-washing story: the old Patriarch is divested of his gold and white robes and girds himself with a towel. He washes the feet of the twelve 'disciples' before him; then three move apart and pretend to sleep, refusing to be awakened by the Patriarch. The feet-washing water is finally sprinkled over the crowd.

The Armenian feet-washing ceremony is more elaborately staged. A blue curtain is drawn aside to reveal the twelve 'apostles' (one usually an Anglican member of the clergy) sitting, somewhat incongruously, on bentwood chairs. The Armenian priests wear high peaked black hoods in the shape of Mount Ararat, situated in their original home Armenia, now a part of Russia. Their vestments are pink or blue and richly embroidered. They hold crosses and candles. Only the right foot is lightly washed and then anointed from butter, again representing Mount Ararat in shape. The choir sings beautifully and all is quiet and reverent.

Good Friday, from an early hour, sees solemn processions along the Via Dolorosa, the Way of Sorrows, stopping at each Station of the Cross. Sometimes, a great wooden cross is carried and there is often competition for the honour of carrying it. I always found most moving the place where Veronica stepped forward and wiped Our Lord's brow with her handkerchief – a non-Biblical story, but quite credible.

On Good Friday night, a deeply moving service, Burial Service, takes place at the Russian Orthodox Cathedral. The intoning of Old Slavonic and the rich deep notes of their funeral chants, including the 'Hymn of the Myrrh-bearing Women', evoke the greatest sense of grief. The priests are clad in black and silver and finally, they process to the Royal Doors, which are slowly opened. Aloft is carried an effigy of Christ wrapped in a white shroud, covered with a black velvet pall. The mourning people follow. As the moon shines down the night, too, is black and silver, dark with sorrow, but hinting at the light to come. The procession circles the cathedral three times and then the Royal Doors re-open, again the Hymn of the Myrrh-bearing Women is sung, the winding-sheet is taken back to the 'Sepulchre'. Old and New Testament readings follow and the service ends with a blessing.

The culmination of Holy Week draws near. On Saturday comes the ecstatic celebration of the Holy Fire. This service symbolises the Resurrection, when Christ, the Light of the World, issued from the tomb. We are in the Church of the Holy Sepulchre. The tomb of Christ, the Edicule, stands in the centre. A great crowd fills the Rotunda, seething and milling to and fro and by no means silent. Everyone carries a white candle, some decorated, some large, some small, but they are not yet lit and the light in the church is very dim. I have a reserved place on a dais near a Greek princess, but the crush has no thought of royalty and the dais is soon invaded. Some of them have been waiting all night; can you wonder if they are impatient for the Resurrection of the Saviour? – or the excitement that goes with it. To me, they are a hallowed throng, although some have likened them to a football crowd. Boys hang from the scaffolding above and babies sit on shoulders. (The Holy Land is also a homely land.) The first procession enters, followed by another and another and another. Greek Orthodox, Armenians, Copts and Syrians take part and Abyssinians are guests of the Copts. Sistras tinkle, ululations rise and fall, banners of every colour unfurl above the crowds. There are priestly head-dresses of every shape and bulbous patriarchal crowns bejewelled with fortunes. The richest of robes are worn by the poorest of monks. Each church finds its own small allotted space of floor, except one that has to resort to the balcony. The atmosphere is tense and excitement rises to fever point as Greek patriarch and Armenian bishop, both bearing large candles, enter the Edicule. There is a hush in the expectation as we wait in profound suspense for the miracle, the coming of the Holy Fire, the coming of the Light of the World. There are small circular apertures (like port-holes), one on each side of the Edicule. At last, from the Greek side, a torch comes through, then, almost instantly, the other from the Armenian side.

The most faithful of the faithful believe this to have come from heaven. Bells ring out in thunderous peals. The crowd surges forward and candle after candle is lit till the whole building is ablaze with light. "Christos aneste, Christos aneste!" The cry rises to the rafters. "The Lord is risen". The Easter joy is overwhelmingly expressed in light and sound. The Greeks take their torch of Holy Fire to their chapel and the Armenians likewise. Once they used to take it as far as Russia. There are more processions to follow, but at last the crowd begins to disperse, each carrying his flame of Holy Fire. The Greek princess's white dress is bespattered with candle grease, but she looks as exultant as all the others. Truly, we have seen a miracle – if only the miracle that has preserved us from fire! Seriously, I am not among those who reject this ceremony as a religious service. I prefer to come away thinking of W.B Yeats' words in "Sailing to Byzantium".

> Sages standing in God's holy fire
> As in the gold mosaic of a wall
> Come from the holy fire, perne in a gyre[4]
> And be the singing-master of my soul
> Consume my heart away

On Saturday night, we move on to the roof of the Holy Sepulchre where the Abyssinians, unable to hold on to their right to a place within the building, now have their chapel and their little beehive dwellings. They are poor, but on this night they are rich as they conduct their strange ceremony of 'Searching for the Body of Christ.' I sat on a wall and peered into a large old brocade tent, the size of a marquee. Everywhere, there were Abyssinians in almost barbaric splendour, priests in magnificent vestments; Kavasses, again in their embroidered uniforms and with swords at their sides, as they stamped and stomped their staves on the ground. A kaleidoscope of flame red, emerald green, blues, purples, stripes, near tartans, moved before our eyes. Priests wore spiked golden crowns and children imitations of them. The Aboune (Abbot) was a solemn figure weighed down by a yet more splendid, golden, bejewelled crown. Candles flickered

---

[4] 'Perne in a gyre' – "The image is of a shuttle revolving round and up the wall of time, in an upward spiral movement."

in the breeze, monks rhythmically beat silver-rimmed drums and shook the tinkling, rattling silver sistra; a jangling bell began to toll and a procession formed as the chanting became a plaintive, mournful wail.

Umbrellas are a symbol of honour to the Abyssinians and, as we moved to a higher viewpoint, we looked down on a slowly moving series of circles, blue, red, green, yellow, heavily embroidered with gold and silver filigree and sparkling in the glittering candlelight. There was an other-worldly mysterious atmosphere about the circling movements of the monks as they set out under the light of the moon in their ritual search for the body of Christ. The Aboune intoned the gospel story. Four times, the monks circled the Cupola of St. Helena's Chapel (which is below in the Holy Sepulchre Church). They swayed and gyrated as their search became frenzied and despairing. At last they returned, dejected, to the brocaded pavilion; their dirge grew more plaintive and mournful, then stopped. Now they were to wait in their sadness till the joy of Easter morning, when they would be as exuberant as they had been abject.

I have read several accounts of this service. There seems to be some variation from year to year and reactions to it all vary, but there is a simplicity of heart at the centre of it and a sincerity which is appealing. It is possible to go to an Abyssinian Easter service, but I never managed to do so. It is held in their cathedral, not far from St. George's Cathedral.

I have told you of the simple Easter service I attended in Ain Karim. Another year, I went very early to the Russian Cathedral. The service begins at 1 a.m. and goes on till 5 a.m. I am not sure that I went to my bed at all that night! I entered into a glorious golden morning. The doors of the Iconostasis (screen) were wide open. Light flooded everywhere. Lighted candles were carried in procession and the priests' vestments were gleaming white and richly gold embroidered. "Christos Aneste" (Christ is Risen) was the exultant cry; everyone turning and repeating it to friend and neighbour. These words, deeply moving, were sung most beautifully:

> *The Angels in Heaven*
> *O Christ our Saviour*
> *Sing Thy Resurrection*
> *And do Thou enable us on earth*
> *To glorify Thee with a pure heart.*

After this, I went to our own Anglican Easter communion in St George's Cathedral.

In Jerusalem, especially at Easter, I found a fundamental unity of faith. Let us never iron out the differences in worship. What a joy there is in the variety of life.

❖ ❖ ❖

More About Churches

Now, like an over-enthusiastic guide, I am saying to myself, "What have I left out?" Where else should I be taking you?" If you have had enough, just drop out. In trying to read all that I have written, you have an advantage. You don't have to go on till you drop. (That has sometimes happened to me). You can just look at the chapter headings and be selective. Metaphorically return to your hotel and have a rest.

For those who are not exhausted, there are several places I would like you to see and then I think I shall leave you. I am imagining that these are my last few days in Jerusalem. I ask myself, "Where are my favourite haunts? Where are the places I should have another look at?" Without intending to make it so, I find that several places I want to revisit are those where Jesus spent his last hours of freedom: – the Coenaculum, the Mount of Olives and Gethsemane. But I have just remembered that, although I have introduced you to a number of churches, I have not taken you to St. George's, where I worshipped regularly.

The Anglican Church began its work in the Holy Land about 1823. In 1833, it purchased the property now known as Christ Church, in the Old City. The Jerusalem Bishropric was founded in 1841 and its first Bishop in Jerusalem, Bishop Alexander, a Jewish convert, took up residence near Christ Church in 1842. British connections with Palestine had begun through trade, as in India. Turkish rule did not finally cease till 1917, when Allenby's troops were victorious on that long famous battle site of Megiddo. I have already told you of Allenby's unassuming entry at the Jaffa Gate and his first speech, benevolent and promising complete tolerance. Our Church has always done much to bring all the people and all the churches and religious foundations together. The Bishops I knew often played a conciliatory part when differences arose.

One of the values I brought back with me from Palestine was not just tolerance of other Christian ways of worship, but delight in them. The wonderful variety of creation and of human existence already meant much to me. I soon became convinced of the naturalness, even the desirability of different approaches to God and different forms of worship in keeping with the differences of birthright and culture which we enjoy. God must love variety: no two people are alike, nor animals (each zebra or giraffe has different markings). When we speak of people's 'differences', we should not be speaking of dislikes and friction, but of love and joy. Of course, human weaknesses and wickedness may hinder this ideal response. Our faith should make us seek to repair such damage and reconcile wherever we go. Missionary endeavour as I saw it meant creative co-operation, only constructive criticism and constant compassion.

St. George's Cathedral is a small 19th century Gothic building with a courtyard, a garden, a Bishop's residence, a Hostel for pilgrims and guests, a secondary school for boys and St. George's College. This complex grew up gradually and is situated on the outskirts of the city on the Nablus Road. Depending on my Boarding House duties, I used to go to early Communion before breakfast and/or to the principal morning service, which was then Mattins, and sometimes to Evensong as well. We walked to church; a pleasant walk: I remember only one slight disturbance (of which I think I have spoken already), the braying of a donkey. A colleague was not so lucky. In 1947, two of the staff were walking to church, as we did, when shots rang out. One of my friends lost her life and, in subsequent reports, the journalist got wrong nearly everything he said about her! Father forgive them – mistaken identity? Does it matter? A wasted life – the waste goes on. Dorothy Norman was the colleague with her and she escaped to uphold Jerusalem Girls' college to the end of the Mandate.

St George's Cathedral, Jerusalem

As I write, Israel's celebration of 50 years of statehood has provoked new disturbances and peace and reconciliation with the Arabs seem as far away as ever. Jesus wept ...

A few more words about our bishops. The second was, I think, Bishop Gobat, who founded another school for boys, named after him. Our bishop when I arrived, was George Francis Graham Brown, a much loved man, quiet, unassuming, truly humble in himself, but with a right sense of the dignity and responsibility of his office. His achievements, of which he never spoke, included coaching Oxford College eights.

He never spared himself. His wife was a doctor, but not practising, and they had one son. We younger members of staff did not find conversation easy when invited by the Graham Browns, but kindness was always there. It was a terrible day when news suddenly came that the bishop had been killed at a level crossing.

Getting new bishops out from England was as difficult as getting teachers. That was an advantage to us, for our new bishop was appointed very quickly; our Archdeacon. Weston Henry Stewart took over very smoothly at what would have been a difficult time for a newcomer. Bishop Stewart had just about every gift a bishop needs. He had high intellectual abilities; he was a scholar of St. Paul's School and of Oriel College, Oxford. He had great administrative ability. He saw clearly what any situation needed; he had the courage to take decisions and act, always with kindly consideration. He was a gifted preacher in English and Arabic, with a deep interest in people at every level. He and his wife remained in Jerusalem when Jews and Arabs were fighting and they helped those who suffered from the conflict in every way possible. They were delightful people to be with and were greatly loved in the Holy Land and in the Peterborough district after retirement from Jerusalem. I think it was Bishop Stewart, with his administrative ability, who saw that, as Anglicanism and bishoprics spread in the Middle East, more co-ordination was desirable. This led to the next bishop in Jerusalem becoming Archbishop over a wide area.

Angus Campbell MacInnes was appointed to this office. He had known Jerusalem since boyhood, for his father, Rennie MacInnes had been bishop before Graham Brown.

After his education in England, in 1932 he came with his friend Michael Gresford-Jones as a missionary teacher. He taught at the Jerusalem Men's College while his friend taught at St. George's School. After a few years, they both returned to Britain for ordination. I never knew Michael Gresford-Jones, but I knew his father when I was a student in Liverpool. Michael's mother and father were very kind to me. His father was Bishop of Warrington. He kindly acted as a referee for me when I applied for my Jerusalem post. You may have read this in an earlier chapter. I like all these little links that make the world a small place. It is amazing how chains of friendship are woven about us. Campbell MacInnes became Bishop of Bedford before he came to Jerusalem again as Archbishop and Michael Gresford-Jones became Bishop of St. Albans. A friend of mine, lecturing at a training college in Bedford, knew them both and worked with them on church committees. Campbell MacInnes had become Archdeacon under Bishop Stewart, but had to return to Britain for medical treatment, after being wounded at the 1948 battle between Jew and Arab. He was greatly welcomed to the Holy City as Archbishop; almost, but never quite, restored to health.

The MacInneses were both delightful people, gentle kindly, able, wise, sensible and joyful. Mrs MacInnes had the very appropriate name of Joy. They had to leave eventually, as health problems became greater. In our days in Jerusalem, there had been an Army Chaplain, admired and liked by Frank, who had also become a friend of the MacInneses. He was Joe Fison, who later became Vicar of Great St. Mary's in Cambridge. (I remember our having tea with him in the Cambridge Senate House, not usually open to the public). Joe moved on to become Bishop of Salisbury and Campbell joined him there in retirement. He shared many duties while the ultimate responsibility was, of course, Joe's. Joe was a very hard worker; a little relief for him was a very good thing. He died relatively young.

The last British bishop in Jerusalem was Bishop Appleton. I did not know Bishop Appleton, who came after Campbell MacInnes, but Bishop Appleton's writings and prayers have helped me.

I learnt from Bishop Appleton's obituary that he had had perhaps the most varied and courageous career of any of the British Bishops in Jerusalem. I wish I had known him. The obituary said that he was universally admired for his wisdom, prayer and pastoral sensitivity. In reading of his career and following his books of prayer, I feel sure that he had great humility. From humble beginnings in Windsor, he reached Selwyn College, Cambridge, trained for the ministry at St. Augustine's College, Canterbury and, after a brief curacy in Stepney, went to Burma. Forced to leave by the Japanese invasion in 1941, he went to India, compiled books on the Burmese language and returned to Burma after the war to be director of Public Relations. In 1947, he returned to England to be a Vicar in Middlesex and Secretary of the Conference of British Missionary Societies and promoted Christian literature overseas. He then worked at Cricklewood and St. Bololph's, Algate. He became deeply involved in Christian/Jewish relations and was made Archdeacon of London and Canon of St. Paul's. Then he went to be Archbishop of Perth in western Australia. After six years, he moved to Jerusalem to be Archbishop there. In retirement, he helped at St. Michael's, Cornhill and finally retired to Oxford. Among other writings, he edited the Oxford Book of Prayer and wrote a 'devotional and reflective' autobiography entitled 'Unfinished', which I want to read. Only Christ could say, "It is finished." Most lives just stop. (I am sure I shall leave a lot of loose ends from my Golden Ball when I go!)

No more about Bishops! I only want to say that all these men gave me an ideal view of bishops – godly men and Fathers in God. Later in life, I have not found all bishops so near to sainthood, but as most of them now only come over to me framed by the media, that may be the reason why.

What is a collective noun for Bishops? Is it a Bench? A Cathedra? – a bevy! I have one more Bishop in my collection. Bishop Kenneth Cragg. I was in Jerusalem when he and his wife, even younger than I, came to work in Beirut. I met them once or twice when they visited Jerusalem. Kenneth Cragg has become the authority on Christian/Muslim relations. He is a great Arabic and Arab scholar. The Craggs became very friendly with my Haifa friend, Catherine Lacey. She stayed with them when Kenneth was made Warden of St. Augustine's College in Canterbury, which trained men from overseas and for overseas work. My friend Elizabeth Nixseaman's father, Canon France, had been a predecessor in that office. Just another little link! Our Rector, when I was a schoolgirl in Canterbury, lived in another part of the Abbey building. Our church, St. George's, was demolished and St. Augustine's was almost bombed. My father's cousin, who lived nearby, had his house destroyed and his wife was killed. My old Canterbury home was also flattened. (Thankfully, my parents had moved away). Jerusalem was almost peaceful; Canterbury was in the front line in 1939-45. How lucky I was, in a strange place, leading an uninterrupted, ordinary life.

I must now return to my original intention for this chapter. I loved walking in or around Jerusalem. I think I must have been in a bus or a taxi occasionally, but I only remember using transport when going farther afield. Many people, before leaving Jerusalem for good, want to ascend the Mount of Olives once more, but before doing that, I am going to take a quick look at the Coenaculum and the Church of the Dormition, close by.

The Coenaculum was in the possession of the Moslems when I was there, and probably still is. The Moslems and the Jews regard this spot as the site of the Tomb of David but to Christians it is the site of the Last Supper and where Christ washed the feet of his disciples and also where the fire of Pentecost descended. There is uncertainty about more than one Biblical site and the alternative to this one is the little church of St. Mark, held by the 'Assyrians', or Syrians, which was one of the earliest places we visited. Generally, it is considered that the Coenaculum has the stronger claim.

'Coenaculum' can be translated 'dining-room'. The Upper Room is a large room where many could have been having supper but, of course, the building is not the one Jesus was in. It belongs, it is said, to Crusader times, replacing an earlier building. I confess it is not one of my favourite sites, in spite of the importance of the Last Supper and the mandate given there.

I suppose as Jesus drew towards the end of His life, He would, like many of us, often have thought of His mother. The Church of the Dormition is the memorial to the 'falling asleep of Our Lady'. I like that. There is peace in it, which we all seek. The tomb of Mary is in Orthodox hands in the Valley of Gethsemane. The Dormitian Church is Latin (RC), built in 1898 on land bought for the German members of the Benedictine Order. It is a circular church with a cupola, the lesser dome you see at some distance from the Dome of the Rock in the panoramic photographs of Jerusalem.

Around the rim of the Dome inside the church are the opening words of the Magnificat "My soul doth magnify the Lord" inscribed in Latin. The patron saint of the Benedictines is the soldier, St. Martin; he has an altar in the church and there are also a number of chapels around the circle. In the crypt below, there is a recumbent effigy of Mary and a chapel to the Holy Ghost, where a service, radiant in flame colours, is held at Whitsuntide.

I visited this church several times attending services and delighting in the singing. I find something very moving and uplifting in plain song (Gregorian chant).

There is another church that comes to mind in thinking of the end of Jesus' life, another modern church, also Latin, built in the 1930's, St. Peter in Gallicante, the 'church of the cock-crowing' which reminds me of Peter's three denials. Cocks can be brightly coloured and beautiful. This church is also brightly coloured; there is difference of opinion on how beautiful it is. But it is a good place for a meditation on one's own faith, steadfastness and courage and how Peter did courageously reform to become a rock of faith – even unto death. Do not give in to your own weakness in the first place, but if you do, rise again (the cock will crow again tomorrow); do not submerge yourself in remorse, rise again to better things, to fresh endeavour: such are the thoughts 'in Gallicante'.

Grotto, Gethsemane.

16. Jericho and Environs

"And Joshua scored seven rounders at Jericho." What do you think of that for a modern version of the Bible? It was told to me as a true quotation from a small child's rendering of the Bible story. When I first saw the ruins of Old Jericho, what immediately struck me was how small they were. Even I might have circled that pile of old rubble seven times. Sir Flinders Petrie was one of the archaeologists who had worked at Jericho. We often saw his widow in Jerusalem. I frequently wondered if she had a sense of humour and would have enjoyed the rounders story. Wonderful archaeological work has been done in Palestine, particularly since it became Israel. Between old discoveries, tree planting and new building, I wonder how much I would recognise if I returned. Some archaeology leaves me cold, but I warm to enthusiasm when things of beauty are revealed. I found beauty in the Jericho oasis and surrounding desert.

Jericho Palms

One Christmas time, I had a holiday in Jericho with Helen Gardner, who was down from Turkey. At that time of year, the weather was ideal, warm but never too hot, as it would become as the year wore on. (Jericho is about 20 miles from Jerusalem and about 4,000 ft. below it. On the Mount of Olives, one is about 2,700 ft. above sea level and the Dead Sea, which is not far from Jericho, is 1,292 ft. below sea level).

We stayed in a small guest house, virtually a private house. We were made very comfortable and were well fed. We could walk to Old Jericho about a mile southwards and could easily visit the Mount of Temptation and the Monastery of St. George on the edge of the desert. I understand that women are not admitted to this monastery, but I have a recollection of climbing up to a monastery built into a cliff side; the cliff side of the Mount of Temptation. This was on another occasion and, if my memory serves me aright, the last part of the ascent was sheer rock face where an obliging monk let down a basket into which one somehow clambered and then he worked the attached ropes to haul one up; a sort of reversal of St. Paul's experience in being let down over the walls of Damascus. When I got to the top, all I remember is that I had interrupted the monk in his making of bread. I suppose the going down would have been even more Pauline. Perhaps this was all a dream; memory plays its tricks in the desert, even more than anywhere else!

Rockface Monastery. Such buildings can be seen on the Mount of Temptation and elsewhere in desert situations

Jericho is said to rival Damascus in age. Damascus claims to be the oldest continuously-settled city, 7,000 years old. Some archaeologists think Jericho is 10,000 years old or more. From this long history, there are at least some remains more tangible than the foundations of 1,200 BC (or is it 1,400 BC?). There is an Ommayed Palace of the 7th century AD, built for the Caliphs of Damascus to come down to in the winter (like me) to enjoy the balminess of Jericho. Something of the opulence of this Hisham Palace can still be imagined: great columns, ornamental stone window decorations and a beautiful Tree of Life mosaic in the Bath House.

Part of the wall of the ruined Hisham Palace, Jericho

Hisham palace, Jericho Stone framed window

The oasis town of Jericho was like an emerald jewel set in the golden sands of the desert. When the beauty of Nature's infinitely varied green and fruitfulness stirs the imagination, the poetry of Andrew Marvell comes to mind. He might have been writing of Jericho and not Bermuda.

> *"He hangs in shades the orange bright*
> *Like golden lamps in a green light*
> *And does in the pomegranates close*
> *Jewels more rich than Ormus shows*
> *He makes the figs our mouths to meet*
> *And throws the melons at our feet."*
> *...*
> *"No white nor red was ever seen*
> *So amorous as this lovely green*

comes from another poem describing the garden of Eden, not so far removed from the oasis of Jericho. I can't resist the aptness of one more quotation:

> *The luscious clusters of the vine*
> *Upon my mouth do crush their wine*
> *The nectarine, and curious peach,*
> *Into my hands themselves do reach:*
> *Stumbling on melons, as I pass,*
> *Insnar'd with flowers, I fall on grass.*

Figs and oranges I remember especially and fresh dates; the oranges were filled with distilled sunshine, warm to the touch and soothing to the taste buds. Palm trees were all around, tall and graceful, sometimes swishing in the winds. Jericho is called 'City of Palms'.

Jericho is the perfect oasis, but often what appears to be an oasis proves to be a mirage. I have been wondering how many an oasis in the mind may be a mirage. It is a memory related to the Jericho and desert area that makes me say this. You will have heard of the Dead Sea Scrolls, discovered by a shepherd boy amusing himself by throwing stones into a cave, not so far from Jericho. This find led to the exciting discoveries of Biblical scrolled manuscripts and the excavation of the whole area around Masada. My memory tells me that one morning, when I was in Haifa in 1945, we heard of the boy's discovery and discussed it round our dining table. But a short while ago, I read that the discovery took place in 1947 and by that time I was back in Britain! In imagination, I had been there. So can you believe anything I tell you? I think you can but, as I warned you in my preface "memory plays us tricks!" True to experience is Mnemosyne, but not always quite accurate on facts. Her offspring are the Muses, who use memory in creation and make things memorable, to give us long-lingering, timeless delights.

On our way back to Jerusalem, we will stop for a moment at the old Khan, or inn, a place for watering the camels. It is said to be the scene of the story of the Good Samaritan. What we call a parable is probably based on a true experience.

The River Jordan

But, before leaving the area around Jericho, let us go down to the Jordan. We can see the place where John the Baptist anointed Jesus; we may see the river looking murky, but people buy bottles of Jordan water and take it home for baptismal purposes. We may also see some kind of modern baptism in the Jordan. Once, I went on to the Allenby Bridge and there were some young soldiers having buckets of water poured over their heads; were they receiving a new baptism or simply cooling down? Allenby brought freedom (from Turkish rule); perhaps it is a pity his name is linked to this bridge, where soldiers now too often have to enforce border restrictions. I believe the name has now been changed.

Having been to the Dead Sea on an earlier occasion, we might now have time to take a distant look at the isolated monastery of Nebi Musa (The Tomb of Moses), sacred to the Muslims who, since the 19th century, have kept a Feast of Nebi Musa about the same time as Passover and Easter.

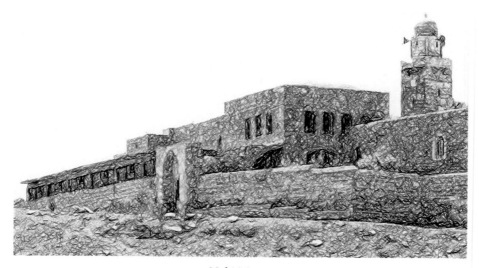

Nebi Musa.

Finally, let me tell you a fragment of history that might be taken romantically or cynically. Mark Antony, liking the 'City of Palms', that is Jericho, presented it to Cleopatra who, growing tired of it (or of Antony?) sold it to Herod the Great. He made it the site of his winter residence and died there in 4 BC. Places outlive people.

17. Hezekiah's Tunnel

Hezekiah, Hezekiah
Conaniah, Benamiah, Mattaniah,
Why didn't you build your tunnel straight?
(Of course, we are telling you much too late)
Why didn't you build the roof much higher?
O Azariah, Ismashaiah,
O Hezekiah, Hezekiah

> **A jingle of Biblical names of kings and workers to chant in the tunnel, to keep away evil spirits!**

"*And the rest of the acts of Hezekiah, and all his might, and how he made a pool and a conduit and brought water into the city; are they not written in the book of the chronicles of the kings of Judah?*"

> *Groping along the tunnel step by step*
> *He winked his prying torch with patching glare*
> *From side to side, and sniffed the unwholesome air*
> **Siegfried Sassoon**

Some of my army friends invited me, among others, out for an evening – not to a good dinner at the King David Hotel, but to Hezekiah's Tunnel. Who would want to spend the evening in a dark, underground tunnel, running with water, that would not merely rise above ankles, but might come up to one's waist. H.V. Morton, writing in 1934, said "It is wet, messy and dangerous." One man said that he would take him to one end of the tunnel and then go to the other end and wait for H.V Morton's body to come out. H.V. Morton also said that the tunnel had been discovered by accident (rather like the Dead Sea Scrolls). Two boys had been playing, discovered the tunnel and managed to crawl through it and come out alive. The boys might not previously have heard of the tunnel, but actually, its existence had been known for centuries. In the 1940's, army people trained to endure physical hardship took to going through the tunnel. It became one of the "things to do". I scarcely regarded it as that but, even though I

knew that army women had found it less than agreeable, I accepted my invitation, for few evenings could have greater historical significance or Biblical authenticity. If someone had told me, as I later read, that the tunnel was full of rats, bats and evil spirits, I might have cancelled my acceptance; instead I was encouraged to 'take the chance'. Before going, I read my Bible, not because I feared the worst, but just to verify the facts (I have had to do a lot of that in writing up these memories of nearly 60 years ago!).

Here is the Biblical account: 2 Chronicles 32:2-4 "And when Hezekiah saw that Sennacherib was come, and that he was purposed to fight against Jerusalem, he took counsel with his princes and his mighty men to stop the waters of the fountains which were without the city; and they did help him. So there was gathered much people together, who stopped all the fountains and the brook that ran the land, saying, 'Why should the kings of Assyria come and find much water'." After that, I regarded my evening as a kind of pilgrimage, a thanksgiving for water, not as plentiful in Palestine as in Britain.

Siloam's inscription from Hezekiah's Tunnel

The stone bearing the celebrated Siloam inscription was discovered in 1880 on the south wall of the tunnel near the Pool opening. Above, the six lines of beautifully carved Hebrew characters are clearly shown from a sequence. They are thus translated; (1) behold the excavation! Now this had been the history of the excavation. While the workmen were still lifting up (2) the axe, each towards his neighbour, and while three cubits still remained to (cut through, each heard) the voice of the other who called (3) to his neighbour for there was an excuse in the rock on the right hand (and on the left). And on the day of the (4) excavation the workmen struck, each to meet his neighbour axe against axe, and there followed (5) the

waters from the spring to the pool for a thousand two hundred cubits .....
(6) of a cubit was the height of the rock over the heads of the workmen.

Were those ancient soldiers defeated because an angel contrived it, or because they were made helpless by illness, or because the lack of water helped to spread their illness, or simply because they had no water. (My husband, who fought in the Western Desert not long before I met him in Jerusalem, has often said "Did we defeat Rommel, a great general, because we had four mugs of water a day and they had only two for all their needs?").

So I would be paddling back to the 7th century BC. My soldiers were in merry mood. My memory fails me on two points: Did I wear shorts? I had first worn shorts in the early 1930's at a school camp (knee length khaki!). We were almost pioneering 'trousers for women'!. But if I wore them in Hezekiah's Tunnel, I don't think I have ever worn them again. When we reached our starting point, off came shoes or sandals, to be worn round the neck; then we started squelching along.

The other thing I cannot remember is, which end did we begin? I think it was from the Gihon Spring end, outside the walls; the other end is at the village of Silwan, in the Pool of Siloam. At both ends, women go up and down steps to wash clothes or collect water in jars, or tannekies (petrol tins). This is one reason for the tunnel expedition taking place at night; so that the silt stirred up by paddling can settle before the women's day begins.

If it had not been for our good company, it would have been a very eerie experience. Most of us carried candles, but there was at least one good-sized torch. The flickering light of the candles added to the spookiness, but the torches were reassuring. They brought the 20th century into the past. Everything was crooked, angular, askew. You couldn't really be certain of anything; sometimes the roof was high, then it became so low that we were bent in two in order to get through. The tunnel was always narrow, but some parts were narrower than others; sometimes we rubbed against the damp walls. Sometimes underfoot was squelchy and muddy, sometimes like treading on soft sand; then a sudden steep bit, knobbly, rocky, toe-cutting. One could easily trip or stumble. Fortunately, none of our party ever fell; the men were very chivalrous, with a ready hand to help; even ready, I believe, chivalrously to save any collapsing female. Story has it that on another occasion the most aggressive woman sergeant collapsed, screeching for help – to general amusement! (Details below!)

The most exciting point when the tunnel was being cut was where the men working from one end eventually met those working from the other. There was an angular kink more or less at this point, indicating they couldn't get it quite right; they were in danger of missing. At one time, there was an inscription in Hebrew on the wall (said to have been discovered by the two boys from Bishop Gobat school). The crucial point of meeting is described: "When the excavators had struck pick against pick, one against the other, the waters flowed from the spring (Gihon) to the pool (Siloam)". The tunnel is about a quarter of a mile long; I confess there were times when it seemed much longer. It was good to come out into the moonlight, even though we had been untroubled by rats or bats and nothing ghoulish had dared to assail such a lively, laughing invasion. Behind my giggling, I had prayed; "From ghoulies and ghosties and long leggity beasties – Good Lord deliver us!" Perhaps that had helped!

I cannot say that I enjoyed this expedition wholeheartedly, but at least I did not emulate one woman member of that completely army group who visited the tunnel on another occasion. As they neared the end of the tunnel, an ample stentorian female sergeant let out a cry of terror and collapsed into the arms of her equally ample and stentorian male counterpart, thus blocking the way out of the tunnel and causing a uniformed queue to build up in the murky waters behind her. Her usual 'popularity' was not enhanced by that military exercise!

18. The Boarding House and Beyond!

I feel them cling and cleave to me
As vines going eagerly up; they twine
My life with other leaves; my time
Is hidden in theirs, their thrills are mine
   W H Auden

I liked the boarding house from the moment I saw it. The building had the solidity and simple dignity of all good Arab architecture. The thick stone walls and vaulted ceilings kept it cool and pleasant in hot weather and kept some of the cold out in winter. From the main doors, one entered into a large, stone floored hall, off which all the rooms opened. Upstairs followed the same basic plan. Downstairs, there was a very large room serving the boarders for dining, for leisure, for homework time and Sunday letter writing. Or was the dining room separate? I'm not sure. Opposite was a large kitchen area. There were one or two staff bedrooms, an office room and a little chapel. Upstairs provided the dormitories, bathrooms and showers, a small sick room, a store and one or two more staff bedrooms. The large central open space provided for more boarder activity, domestic or recreational, in an informal way. There was a balcony over the front porch where a few staff or senior girls could sit.

The building was airy and comfortable and I was never aware of noise from fifty-odd boarders being overpowering. No need to suppress natural enjoyment! (Anything beyond that would certainly have been controlled, and <u>easily</u> controlled.) I remember only once wondering what all the noise was about and that was quite early in the morning. I discovered that it was just the Arab Housekeeper giving her orders for the day! Arabs (like many Europeans) can be excitable. I have seen it in another country that I love, Italy. Quickly up and usually quickly down. Short storms followed by beaming sunny smiles in no time.

Our days began early; no hardship in a sunny climate. In the Boarding House, 5.30 a.m. was not unusual. All staff were wakened with early morning tea and hot water for washing. We still had the old-fashioned washstands with basin and ewer. Unless on duty with the boarders, the staff breakfasted in the Staff House, an excellent breakfast; leban (yogurt) or winter porridge followed by a good variety of cooked bacon, eggs, etc., toast and marmalade, tea or coffee.

The Boarding House – Beginning and Ending

Boarding House breakfast was entirely Arab – leban, goat's cheese, hard and white, or lebaneh, i.e. soft cheese balls in olive oil, debbis sometimes (a kind of syrup made from grapes) apricot preserve and fruit, usually the mishmish themselves or, more often, oranges. Not all these appeared on the same day, just the Matron's selection, for the Matron had the last word on food as well as being responsible for health. Now that I have got on to the subject of food, I will complete it. A short while after I arrived in Jerusalem I wrote home: "The food here is really excellent .... We have a few wartime economies, but no shortage of anything. At lunch time, we have Arabic food with the girls, but otherwise English dishes. Our present Housekeeper (who is also Domestic Science Mistress) is leaving to get married in the summer. I hope that her successor is as efficient!" I do not think she had a successor. An English Matron came with nursing qualifications and the Arab (whom I have already mentioned) who mainly looked after cleaning, etc. and Arabic food.

The Headmistress took an interest in Staff House food and was good at training local staff to make dishes she liked. In one letter I said "We did not often get cheese, as Miss C. did not like it." I also expressed the hope that the cheese ration at home still allowed for a little bit for their cat Toby, who was (like the Ain Karim cats – but with better manners!) partial to it. Some Arabic dishes were stuffed vine leaves, aubergines and courgettes, fried or stuffed, meat stews, especially lamb with leban (yoghurt); kibboch, a delicious pounded combination of meat, onions and burghhul, which can be eaten raw but is much better when fried. Okra was a vegetable I grew to like, cooked with tomatoes and onions. Samak (fish) – I don't think we had it often in Jerusalem, but in Haifa I remember the best fish dish I have ever tasted; onions were used in it. Meatballs and lentil or chick pea rissoles often appeared on the menu, as did mejedera (mess of pottage). I cannot think how anyone would want to sell his birthright for that. Esau must have been very hungry indeed! Lentil soup I liked, but mejedera (also largely made from lentils) acquired a flavour which I did not find to my taste; usually I liked the Middle East spicing.

Mishmish (meat with apricots) was a good example of a meat and fruit dish, but I did not taste it often. Some foods had good stories behind them. You may nowadays have heard of Imam Bayildi 'The Imam Fainted' – whether he fainted from delight or when he heard the cost of this dish we do not know; it is not really very expensive, just being stuffed aubergines cooked in olive oil.

Salads, of course, are popular in hot countries (if properly washed – very important). Holidays in Turkey and elsewhere could be almost spoilt if one were told 'No salads; no ice cream' when one would be longing for both. This was an army order during the war.

Tabbouleh is one of the few Arab foods I have served with success at home. It is made of fine burghul (cracked wheat) chopped (spring) onions, parsley and mint, lemon juice, olive oil and seasoning. It is scooped up with vine or lettuce leaves in the East.

Oh, I nearly forgot the omelettes and bread. An Arab omelette is something like the Spanish tortilla. We do not know which came first. Did the Arabs take theirs to Spain or did they bring it away from Spain? The Arab omelette, called 'eggah' is firm and can be cut like a cake. It can have various fillings. A French-type omelette is light and the filling is secondary: the eggah exists for the sake of the filling. It is a wrapper, usually quite thick. It can be eaten cold and is very good on picnics. Arab bread is also often eaten with similar fillings.

In both the Boarding House and the Staff House, we ate English bread, but Arab bread was also served in the Boarding house.

It is interesting that in St. John's gospel 21.5, there is a Greek word, difficult to translate 'prosphagion'. It is still used in Cypriot Greek and is translated IDAK in Arabic. Idak, according to the Arabic dictionary, means 'to season bread with a condiment', but it has been heard used in modern times in the reproachful sentence: "Are you offering me a loaf of bread without an idak?" The idak could be fish (translations of St. John 21.5 assume this) or olives, or hard-boiled egg or thyme and sesame seeds or onions, peppers, pickles, or soft cheese preserved in oil. The nearest we have to this must be a filled roll.

I have enjoyed reading different accounts of bread making. Kinglake gives an early account of bread being made by his followers in the desert:

"The very first baker of bread that ever lived must have done his work exactly as the Arab does at this day. He takes some meal, and holds it out in the hollow of his hands, whilst his comrade pours over it a few drops of water; he then mashes up the moistened flour into a paste, pulls the lump of dough to make it into small pieces, and thrusts them into the embers. His way of baking exactly resembles the craft or mystery of roasting chestnuts, as practised by children; there is the same prudence and circumspection in choosing a good berth for the morsel – the same enterprise and self-sacrificing valour in pulling it out with the fingers."

(I hope you appreciate the comparison. Has central heating killed the joy of roasting chestnuts, as it has killed the joy of toasting bread before a coal fire?)

At the beginning of the 20th century, Gertrude Bell wrote: "I have just been watching my people make bread. Flour was fortunately to be got from the mill below us; they set two logs alight and when they had got enough ashes they made an immense cake, 2 feet across and half an inch thick, of flour and water and covered it over with hot ashes. After a quarter of an hour, it had to be turned and recovered and the result is most delicious – eaten hot; it becomes rather wooden when cold. The flour is very coarse, almost like oatmeal."

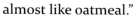

Now, I am sure those of you who are home bakers are longing to make Arab bread!

But I have got to get you away from the desert and back to the Boarding House in Jerusalem.

When I left it, we were talking about food. Now, just a word or two about water. There was always a shortage. The daily bath was 'out'! In the Boarding House, we had a rota for staff and girls alike. In those days, staff preferred baths and girls preferred showers, as being truer to the tradition of most of them to pour water over themselves.

Drinking water had a romantic touch to it, at least for me. In the Boarding House hall stood a very large jar, almost big enough to accommodate a couple of Ali Baba's thieves, or two naughty schoolgirls! It contained, and kept reasonably cool, drinking water. By it, stood a jug, rather like an Arab coffee pot. From time to time, a girl would fill the jug and then throw her head back and let a stream of water fall down her throat. She never touched the spout with her mouth, so that the jug remained hygienic. This was an art I never learnt.

By this time staffing was becoming a problem. Four British staff left to get married, one returned home, risking a sea passage, to care for an ailing mother, Peggy Craig, the school Secretary, moved to a British Council post in Egypt, and Marion Gilmour had transferred to the secretariat, where she did important translation work for the Government. At one point, three new staff were supposed to be coming out from England, but only one eventually came, a Cambridge graduate, but not dedicated to teaching. We discovered that her main reason for applying for the post was to get married to a young army officer stationed in Jerusalem. I remember helping her to dress on her wedding day – and she soon disappeared!

It was a busy life, but enjoyable.

Lucretius, writing long ago, wrote words which I find applicable:

> Thus yesterday, today, tomorrow come,
> They bustle one another and they pass;
> But all our hustling morrows only make
> The smooth today of God.

From 1939 to 1941, life in the Boarding House, as in the school, went smoothly and it seemed as if it would go on forever. There were always fresh plans. The school decided to have a House System and four women saints were chosen for names. I believe the boarders were St. Helena, suitably, as we were only yards from a monastery built on the spot where St. Helena found the trees that provided wood for the Cross. St. Barbara was hitherto a saint unknown to me. I think a third was St. Veronica, whom I have always liked for her little gentle act in wiping Christ's brow as he carried his Cross. Several handkerchiefs are extant. If you doubt them, you are told it was a folded handkerchief and each was one of the folds. St. Margaret might have been the fourth house saint, but my memory fails me.

St. Helena did well in sport and country dance competitions, etc. Dramatics flourished in school and Boarding House. I remember a non-boarder, Batsheva Benjamin, a red-head, as a very creditable Katherine in scenes from "The Taming of the Shrew".

I myself had a prominent part in a Boarding House pageant to celebrate 21 years since the boarders first came. Overleaf is a copy of the opening ceremony in November, 1922.

Miss Irvine was the first House Mistress. She was a redoubtable Presbyterian lady with a heart of gold. I knew her as Head Mistress of a Church Mission to the Jews school in Jaffa. One of my friends on the staff (an Anglo-Arab) had been a pupil under Miss Irvine, who then taught geography at J.G.C. Gaby told me that they were so much in awe of Miss Irvine that if anything amusing occurred, or if Miss Irvine herself made a joke, they would not dare reveal their amusement until she said, "Girls, you may laugh." Gaby shared my regard for Miss Irvine and said that the girls soon came to know her worth. She was always kind to me. I stayed in her school several times and she came to J.G.C. sometimes in the long vacation and ran it as a hostel or conference centre, even doing some of the cooking herself.

FORM OF SERVICE
for the
OPENING OF THE BOARDING HOUSE
of the BRITISH HIGH SCHOOL
(the original name of Jerusalem Girls' College)
By MRS DEEDES
November, 1922

When all have taken their appointed places, the Bishop shall say:
"I shall ask Mrs Deedes to open the door of the Boarding House after the hymn
has been sung."

Then all will take part in the following service:

Bishop : come, ye children, and hearken unto me.
Reply: I will teach you the fear of the Lord.

V. The fear of the Lord is the beginning of wisdom;
R. A good understanding have all they that do thereafter.
V. Them that are meek shall he guide in judgment;
R. And such as are gentle, them shall he learn his way.
V. They that be wise shall shine as the brightness of the firmament;
R. And they that turn many to righteousness as the stars for ever and ever.
V. May our sons grow up as the young plants;
R. And our daughters as the polished corners of the Temple.
V. Except the Lord build the house;
R. Their labour is but lost that build it.

Then all will join in the singing of the hymn:

All things are Thine; no gift have we,
Lord of all gifts, to offer Thee;
And hence with grateful hearts today
Thine own before Thy feet we lay.

Thy will was in the builder's thought;
Thy hand unseen amidst us wrought;
Through mortal motives, scheme and plan,
Thy wise eternal purpose ran.

O Father, deign these walls to bless,
Fill with Thy love their emptiness;
And let their door a gateway be
To lead us from ourselves to Thee.

After the singing of the hymn, Mrs Deedes
will open the door of the Boarding House.

I still remember her curries and her belief in Leban for any tummy problems. After she retired as Head Mistress (the school, like the others, must have ended in 1948), she became Warden/Hostess of St. George's Hostel, part of our Cathedral complex and still a very good place to stay. When Miss Irvine really retired, she came to Scotland and had one of the little houses in Dunkeld, restored by the National Trust.

It was an honour to be asked to play the part of Miss Irvine in the pageant. I could not produce even the trace of a Scottish accent, or really represent her very well, but colleagues said I was more like her than any of the rest of them. This is what I said about it in a letter home:

> "I was on and off the stage a great deal, though being a pageant with tableaux I didn't, thank goodness, have a great deal to learn. I wore a sprigged muslin dress, attached a band to my hair and wore a black hat trimmed with lace and red roses, sitting very flat on my head. My shoes and stockings were white and I carried white gloves, and had a white lace edged handkerchief; all very correct. My winter dress was more sober and, at the beginning of one scene, I sat in lamplight writing a diary and sipping tea, with a shawl about my shoulders and a brilliant tartan rug thrown over my knees."

I wish now that I had been more like Miss Irvine and had kept a diary! It would have been very useful. Her advice I always found very helpful; she was indeed another of Palestine's Redoubtable Ladies.

Catherine Blackwood, who was running the Boarding house at the beginning of the war, announced her engagement in 1941. I was given extra Boarding House duties with a view to taking over from her, really if no-one turned up who was older and more suitable! Soon, I was called Assistant House Mistress and I became House Mistress at the beginning of 1942.

There are a few comments on my new appointment in my letters home:

> "I've get a few grey hairs now. I wonder if I shall be 30 before I return. Everyone here still seems to think of me as very young and, indeed, I don't feel much older, though perhaps I shall do now that I am responsible for the welfare of 52 girls from 9 to 19 years old!"

I was a little anxious about having an English and an Arab matron older than myself, but I said:

> "I think we shall be able to work together satisfactorily" and so we did. The thought of extra work did not seem to worry me. I wrote; "I am not giving up all my teaching. I shall still be teaching English and Latin and also I am very glad that I am keeping my form till the end of the year. I think it is the nicest form I've had and I don't want to lose them." There was still time and energy to do some of the extras. I con-

tinued: "*Last Wednesday I took them all for a picnic to a wood near Bethlehem. After lunch, we walked into Bethlehem and went to see the Church. Jewesses and Moslems all came. If I can fit it in, I am going to take some of them to Jericho before the end of term. Many of them have not been before. The only difficulty about these outings is that most of the Jewesses want to walk miles and many of the Arabs, especially the Moslems, are not used to walking and cannot go nearly so far.*"

Our boarders came from very different backgrounds and one had to meet their individual needs and help them to adapt. Sometimes, I had a special mission to carry out on someone's behalf. I mention one here:

"*On Saturday, I'm going to Bethany to visit an Assyrian whose home is in the Habor at the very north of Syria. Of course, she cannot go home for the short holiday and so she is being lodged in a Russian convent school. She came without a comb, a toothbrush, or the usual underwear, so I've had to get her all her things. I'm taking her summer dresses tomorrow.*" I felt sorry for her, but she seemed pleased by my visit and everyone was being kind to her.*"

From time to time, I could forget my girls (I was not quite a Miss Jean Brodie!). Here is an account of an evening out! "As this is half-term, I've been having quite a good time. Last night, a friend and I went out with two men in the Wiltshire Yeomanry. We had an excellent dinner and then danced at the King David Hotel. When I got back, I found that the door had been bolted, so there was a little excitement over that, but finally we managed to waken someone who let me in. The door is always locked early in the evening, but I had never known it to be bolted before. I think a new maid did it. Another night, we were glad the door was bolted. There came a great hammering on it. Australian hefty men, the worse for drink, wanted to get in. At last they admitted defeat and became profusely apologetic. "Oh, you're nuns, very sorry, very sorry." As they retreated, we laughed. The colleague with me said, "You know, it might be better if we were nuns, and completely single minded." No more visits to the King David! Teatime outings were more frequent than evening ones. I wrote of one:

Two of us went out to Ramallah, a very pretty place, to visit some friends. There, we had a most delicious home-made tea, with scones, a kind of local cream cheese, jelly, honey and all kinds of native things. Then we came home with huge bunches of violets. The violets grown here really are marvellous – still heavenly scented.

Our little world was going on serenely; the war seemed to be receding. I wrote again: "I've grown very fond of my boarders and some, at least, seem fond of me! They have given me, or tried to give me this term, flowers, sweets, cakes, books, photographs, paper handkerchiefs (a most thought-ful gift when I had a bad cold) and finally a toy pig and a mouse. The last they made themselves, originally for a competition. I shall treasure them." I also received a pair of the first ever nylons which never wore out. They lasted ten years or more.

But the war was still on and its secondary effects began to tell. On 18th october, 1942, I wrote: "Things begin to get more and more expensive ..... I shouldn't be surprised if one day we too found ourselves having coupons for clothes. We are going to have points for rationing soon. All private cars are now off the roads. So you see, we are getting more like England now. A good pair of shoes these days costs over £3 and dresses only begin to be decent at £6 and coats are £9-£11 or more. I bought one second-hand from Margery Adeney when she left to get married." (what a lovely coat that was, warm and feather light, being made of cashmere or something equally luxurious. Margery had gone to live in Baghdad and then Egypt, where no winter coats would be needed. She invited me to visit them in both places, but getting visas became increasingly difficult.)

The school was hit severely by staffing problems and then by food diffi-culties. On the 14th May, 1942, it came as something of a shock to be told that the School Management Committee had said there must be drastic economies that the war was making necessary. They decided to stop hav-ing separate cooks for staff and girls and to have all meals in the same house at the same time. I wrote: "The Boarding House is to be reduced in size, all the juniors being asked to leave. For some time, we have felt it difficult to have, in rather inadequate buildings, girls of so many different ages and I shall not be sorry to have a completely senior house." Juniors probably suffered most from being far from home. One little girl devel-oped Kleptomania. We found her shoe bag full of tubes of toothpaste and mainly useless things. She needed affection. I normally kept a certain dis-tance, but when I showed her I cared for her with some motherly affection, some of her problems disappeared. I continued, "We may have to have two classrooms in our buildings, which will be a disadvantage." This never hap-pened as far as I can remember. All of these gloomy ideas came as a shock because, not so long before, the Head Mistress had been talking of a se-cond Boarding House, as there were more applications than places. I think she liked change better than I did. She had once had a wall pulled down at one end of the school building and another put up at the other end. I learnt in Jerusalem that change is often embarked upon when the daily round becomes irksome. The chapel was moved from the Boarding House to the school, so that for their evening prayer girls had to go out across the compound, whatever the weather. The vaulted room in the Boarding House had a much more suitable chapel atmosphere. I do not remember everyone eating at the same time in the same place, but there is no doubt that the dragon of restlessness raised its head from time to time, in one way or another and our stability became threatened.

When I began writing this 'chronicle', I decided to put on my rose-coloured spectacles. They seem to have slipped a bit. I'll take them off and tell you that problems increased. Once, I remember the boarders complained to me about their food. I passed on what they said to the Matron, who did not take it well. We were really quite friendly, but although we had no hot words, there were some cooling moments. The assistant Arab Matron/Housekeeper left suddenly. I never knew why.

The Head Mistress must have been feeling the strain, not surprisingly, as she had weathered the Arab Troubles before 1939, and now the war was in an uncertain state and Jewish Troubles were almost certain to break out when peace came. There were some signs of it. I remember going shopping one morning and then finding myself in a crowd of people. A colleague managed to join me as we realised we were caught up in a protest march. (We were quite glad we were sometimes taken for Jewesses.) Somehow, we got separated again, just as we were nearing the corner and I was nearly bayonetted by a very young half-shy, half-frightened British soldier-boy. In the end, the Army let me through after I had declared myself English and told them where I was trying to go. My friend and I had agreed to go our separate ways if necessary. She took the longer route and, I must say, I was glad when I saw her arriving back.

Our school was very near the Jewish Agency; there must have been another political hiccup when we had some function on at the school, for more young soldiers were posted strategically outside it. Some of our refreshments were left over and I liked the common humanity that made two of the Jewish girls say, "May we take some of the left-overs to the soldiers on duty? They look so miserable." I don't remember what happened. I thought if the young soldiers were found chewing sandwiches and cake while on duty, provided by young girls, they might well be 'put on a charge' – no kindness in that.

It must have been early in 1943 that a great tragedy occurred. Our Bishop suffered a terrible accident; he was killed at a railway crossing. He was a man of great sincerity, integrity and humility, while being very conscious of the dignity and the demands of his office. His death meant a great loss for the Middle East. Our Head Mistress, who was a friend of the family, was very shaken. For all of us it was not merely unsettling; it brought about decisive changes. Little time was lost in appointing a new Bishop; our Archdeacon, who had long experience in the diocese, was elevated to the bishopric. We were all relieved and happy at the choice. Very soon, he visited the Head Mistress and soon afterwards we heard that she would be leaving us to go on long leave and then perhaps return as a diocesan Education Adviser. Her successor was soon appointed. Again, no attempt was made to bring out someone from Britain. The new Bishop went to our sister school in Haifa and interviewed three of their senior staff and the English Mistress was chosen to come to Jerusalem. Before I knew where I was, I was asked to transfer to Haifa. I wrote in a letter home: "I have said that I will go, but will not promise more than a year's work there, as I want a bigger change than that ..... I expect I shall like it: most people are very happy under Miss Emery. The Boarding House is going to be closed, partly because of shortage of staff and partly because of food difficulties. I'm not sure whether to be glad or sorry. Really, I am sorry. I think it supplies a need; on the other hand, I think it would only get more and more difficult to run it well."

For some time, I had really been wanting to get home and the restlessness bug had affected me. At the end of 1941, I had written, "My liking for the girls makes me wonder sometimes if I shall stay here always. There is undoubtedly a greater need for teachers here than in England and in peace time, when one could get home every other year, it would be very nice." By 1943, I was thinking differently. There are two references in my letters that made me realise I had been thinking of my next move for some time. Towards the end of the war, there was a general uncertainty and restlessness.

18th October, 1942. "I am wondering very much whether to leave here this year. I like the house-mistressing, but there are things that make me want a change. On the other hand, I know they'll have an awful job to replace me here; of the three staff who were to come out to us, only one has arrived. Of course, if food problems get very bad, then I suppose they will have to close the Boarding House and then I shall feel more free to go."

I had become friendly with someone who had worked in Turkey and she was returning there. In one letter, I said I had been invited to join her there for a holiday. Then in another I was surprised to read that I had been offered a job there. In another, which even more surprised me, I said that I had received a second letter from India. Had they kept in touch with me since I chose to go to Jerusalem, rather than accept a post in India? Did they want me to move on there? Did I want to move on there and perhaps complete that teaching circle round the world I had once dreamed about? No, I wanted my next move to be England. In the meantime, I was destined for Haifa.

I had some qualms about the move, because I was aware that there was an Oxford v Cambridge, Glasgow v Edinburgh, Liverpool v Manchester feeling between Haifa and Jerusalem. I also knew that they had been a more close-knit British staff, with fewer moves and marriages than we had had and there were pros and cons. I then realised that one of my earliest holidays had been spent at E.H.S. A letter dated 14th January, 1940 says, "For a few days in the holidays, Marion Gilmour and I went to Haifa. I stayed at the school with Zena Wood. Several of their staff were there; they were all very kind to me and I enjoyed it. We met a number of people and on New Year's Eve Mrs Stewart, whom Marion had known in Scotland, invited us to dinner. We had a lovely time there. Her husband died some years ago and now she lives with an Arab family by the name of Haddad. We had a grand feast, partly Arab, partly Scottish. The oldest girl of the family ate with us and the two younger ones waited on us. After we had finished the meal, some more friends arrived. Then the three little boys of the family, triplets about 12 years old, came in and solemnly shook hands with us all round. After that, they sat in a row on the sofa and looked quite unnaturally good. Arab children are certainly brought up to have perfect manners in the home and before guests. We saw the New Year in with wine and Christmas cake and then hurried 'home' to get in before 1 o'clock, as there is still a curfew on Haifa and everyone has to be indoors before 1 a.m.

One day, Zena and Marion and I went up Mount Carmel and had a glorious picnic. It looks over the Bay of Haifa and across the Mediterranean – a lovely view".

Before going to Haifa, there came the long vacation – about 3 months. In previous years, part of the summer had been taken up with courses or conferences which I had enjoyed. One year I wrote: "The Summer School for English teachers was very good indeed. The lectures were mostly much better than our University lectures (the lecturers usually came from Beirut University or the British Council). We finished up with a moonlight party. One of our former staff planned a treasure hunt (and covered the garden in V's) which a colleague and I won. Then we did a charade which was a skit on the lectures. It went very well!"

That last year, there were no lectures on Semantics or the Apocrypha or other learned subjects to digest. My efforts of the mind were to be exercised at quite a different level – at the other end of the scale!

"I went to Es Salt, where I had been asked to go to coach the 6 year old daughter of the British doctor there. It would be an economical semi-holiday, as I should be living with the family. I had to be persuaded to go, as I wrote home, "It is something quite new to me to have anyone so young to teach." I am not sure that I taught her very much. She had a very clever father, but learning seemed to have no appeal for her. I am quite sure I looked forward to getting back to teaching senior girls.

I don't think I explored Salt very well, for it never really captured my imagination. I feel it should have done, for it can claim to be the most historic town in Jordan, having been settled since the Iron Age. It claims a moderate climate, plenty of water and fertile soil and is well situated on long established trade routes. Of more interest to many of us will be the fact that it gave its name to the dried grape for which it has been famous – the sultana. I suppose we should spell it 'saltana'. The town is mainly Moslem, but has a large minority of Christians. Generally, they live side by side quite happily.

While I was there, I was struck by one incident that brought home to me how blood-feuds survived then. The doctor came home from the hospital one day looking tired and troubled. He had just discharged a man, having saved his life from a stabbing wound. In bidding him farewell, he asked him what he was intending to do now that he was recovered. "I am going to do to that man what he did to me." The good Christian doctor was disappointed. We can still say today, "Will some people ever learn?"

Every so often in my letters I mentioned stockings. I had come to wearing cotton instead of silk (I darned assiduously) and often wore none at all. Knowing that Salt was largely Moslem, I decided I must wear my stockings. I remember skipping along until I felt very hot and then flinging my arms wide to catch the air; my arms were almost bare. I afterwards learnt that bare legs would not matter, but bare arms were not approved!

The hospital was a Christian foundation. The C.M.S. had established one in 1882. Life in the doctor's house was not spartan, but quite colonial. I remember there was a good deal of well-polished silver, a lot it seemed, for what seemed to me a remote outpost. Afternoon tea was always elegant and quite formal; the silver teapot, etc. always appeared.

Salt was long under Ottoman rule, like so much of the Middle East, but always fiercely independent in spirit. It flourished during the Ummayad period and many notable families built fine houses. It is largely a town that climbs a hillside. Minarets and mosques and a secondary school can be seen and a Christian Church (built in 1869) with a school. (If I remember rightly, one of our J.G.C. staff left to run it.) Salt declined to some extent after World War 1. A new Emirate of Transjordan was created and Abdullah came from the Hejaz with some followers; they unfortunately upset certain local people. Abdullah felt they were not receiving traditional hospitality and decided to transfer the capital to Amman, where it has remained ever since. Amman has become increasingly well-developed and prosperous, while Salt is more or less an appendage to it.

19. Last Thoughts of Jerusalem

My days in Jerusalem were now numbered. When any chapter in one's life is coming to its end, one looks back on it usually with some pleasure and some pain. I shall always consider it a great privilege to have lived and worked in the greatest city in the world, for such it remains, with its three monolithic faiths, whatever human evils, errors or griefs overshadow it. As I was about to leave it, I asked myself what had been my greatest pleasures during the past four years; too many and too varied to sort out and record.

One little pleasure I have not recorded in this story must now be mentioned – it is the donkey. I saw those patient laden beasts befriending men beyond their realisation. I never saw a stubborn one. I often saw a pathetic one. My closest relationship with one was on a Sunday morning, walking to St. George's Cathedral in time for the early service – 7 a.m., I think. The bells were ringing, but there was a strange cacophony. A donkey was braying in unison, or in strong competition. Was he trying to sing; was there something in his ancestral memory that reminded him of a forebear who once carried Our Lord in triumph into the Holy City? G K Chesterton's poem came to my mind. Here is part of it to remind you:

> The tattered outlaw of the earth,
> Of ancient crooked will,
> Starve, scourge, deride me: I am dumb,
> I keep my secret still.
>
> Fools! For I also had my hour;
> One far, fierce hour and sweet:
> There was a shout about my ears,
> And palms before my feet.

I came face to face with the donkey. Was he hungry? Was he praising the Lord in his way? He was certainly not dumb. As quietly and kindly as I could I said, "Do please be quiet." He looked at me and decided to keep his secret once more in silence. Not another sound. He came a little nearer and I patted him goodbye. Just one of those fleeting friendships: but I did send up a prayer for patient donkeys – and their owners.

This is leading up to saying that one of my most memorable Jerusalem outings was a ride on a donkey – by moonlight round the old city walls. I referred to it in one of my letters: "Tomorrow night, I am going for a moonlight donkey ride. I've never been on a donkey yet, so I'm looking forward to the adventure with rather mixed feelings. Tomorrow will be a full day – some lessons and House business in the morning, full rehearsal of school play in the afternoon, a quick tea and then a study group on the Apocalypses of the Old and New Testaments, then out to a science lecture with the boarders and, finally, dinner at the Scottish Hospice, and at 9 p.m. we set out on the donkeys. I hope I shan't fall asleep on mine!"

I didn't fall asleep. I loved it. The paths were narrow and the ground often rocky, but the donkeys were sure-footed. We passed familiar sites and the lady who had organised it all – Miss Padwick, one of the Redoubtables – had brought a delicious picnic. The moonlight was strong enough to serve it and eat it comfortably. There was laughter and there was fun, but there was also at times a poetic feeling; something mysterious, mystical, etheral and timeless. We were one with the past, the changelessness of life; and over all hung the velvety darkness of the sky and the silvery light of the moon. The beautiful opening chapter of St. John came to mind. "The light shineth in darkness; and the darkness comprehendeth it not." I like 'comprehendeth' there, rather than 'overcame', for comprehendeth means also 'understood'; it can also mean 'enveloped'. That night, there seemed a perfect 'understanding' between darkness and light – as the 'Light of the World' understands, comprehends, takes into his power, enfolds in mercy the darkness, the wickedness of the world, and transforms humanity. We have received the Light that lightens the world.

I will not suggest you all read Sir Ronald Storrs' 'Orientations', but instead of trying to convey to you how I felt on leaving Jerusalem, I am going to quote what Storrs wrote when he was leaving that centre of the world (once thought literally to be so, and there is a sign marking the exact spot in the Church of the Holy Sepulchre). I felt much the same as Sir Ronald did, although he had been the most important British person serving the country and I was a very insignificant expatriate, unknown except to a very few people.

"I had always dreaded the day when I should have to leave Jerusalem... On the eve of our going, we climbed the Russian Tower of the Ascension and drank in for the last time that doubly magnificent view: to the east the scarred Wilderness of Zin, for all the world like the dead craters of the moon, the dull strong matrix turquoise of the Dead Sea, the amethystine rampart of Moab and Edom; to the west the walls and battlements encircling domes, towers and pinnacles which, for all their forty sieges and destructions still present intrinsically the distant Jerusalem contemplated and lamented by Christ. A city set in the midst of mountains gaunt, austere, uncompromising, but yet of a perfect distinction and in a

supreme style; of an atmosphere at once thrilling and poignant, which from the first, had taken my heart...

I cannot pretend to describe or analyse my love for Jerusalem. It is not wholly sentimental, aesthetic or religious – still less theological or archaeological; though I hope it contains something of all five. A little perhaps that I had worked and enjoyed and suffered there from the beginning; that I knew the people so well and liked them so much.... Persons of wider experience and more facile emotions have often come there to pray and gone away to mock. For me, Jerusalem stood and stands alone among the cities of the world."

20. Haifa

Haifa Bay from the lower slopes of Mount Carmel

It was about the middle of September, 1943 that I went to Haifa. The school building was not strange to me, as I had already stayed there as a visitor in holiday times. The school was entirely a day school, so it was just one substantial stone building, quite near the road, with a small garden in front of it and a playground at the back. Inside, it was spacious, light and airy, with a fine wide staircase, almost handsome, and sensible for a school. No silence rules were needed. One member of staff could stand at its head on the floor above and all movement could be quiet and orderly without undue restriction. I was still young enough to want to run up those stairs two at a time. After hours, other young colleagues and I often did. During school hours, more mature decorum was observed. I think there were three floors; offices, kitchen quarters, staff dining and sitting rooms were on the ground floor, classrooms on the first floor and staff bedrooms and bathrooms above. All staff bedrooms looked out over Haifa Bay and beyond to Mount Hermon. It was lovely to watch the changing light and snowline on Hermon. There was an enormous flat roof projecting from the first floor, where staff and senior girls often met and chatted.

Our other mountain was Carmel. We had only to cross the road to be at its foot and we climbed up it many times. Many of our girls lived on Carmel and came to school on the local bus. I remember on the lower paths gathering wild narcissus; on the higher paths one could lie on carpets of tiny flowers of all colours and enjoy them as I had enjoyed those in Nazareth. Girls often brought bunches of wild flowers to school.

Not far from us, on the slopes of Carmel overlooking the sea, there was a very special garden and in it you will see a white buildings with a golden cupola, glinting in the sun as brightly as does the Dome of the Rock in Jerusalem. Beneath the Bahai Dome lie the remains of their religious founder. He was executed by the Moslem Turks as a renegade Moslem. He created a gentler, more tolerant, variant from Islam, a religion free from fanaticism. He called himself El Bab – the Gateway – that is the Gateway to God, to communication with the supreme. Bahais believe that all the religions of the world preach the same basic doctrine – love one another. They honour Moses, Christ, Mohammed and Buddha and teach brotherhood and tolerance and would like to have a common world language through which to bring about greater understanding of one another.

The Bahai Dome.

Their garden is a place of great peace. I was told that it was not for sitting in but for walking and contemplating. Sometimes, one would see a white turbaned priest walking with book in hand. There is a library and archive building in one corner of the garden. The garden is a very gracious place, with cypress trees pointing their fingers to heaven, reminding one of a Persian garden, appropriately, as the religion had its origin in Persia. We had several Bahai girls in our school, all of them delightful, with a graceful quietness in their nature. Bahai means 'glory' in Persian. The religion only began in 1850. The Turks tried to eradicate it, executing both its founder and its prophet, whose tomb is in Acre. I remember going there on an outing where the Bahai girls quietly acted as our guides.

A more historic settlement on Carmel was that of the Carmelite order, founded by Barthold of Calabria, a Crusader, in 1155. Then Saladin retook the town; then Richard the Lionheart reversed that; then came a Bedouin rule, made prosperous by trading wheat; then Turks, now more benevolent, and the Carmelites re-established and built a church and monastery near Elijah's Grotto – which goes much farther back in history still, to when Elijah asserted the birth of his God over Baal: I remember lovely red tulips at the Place of Sacrifice.

On quite a different scale, from a little way up Carmel one could see the German Colony with its neat gardens, almost prim in their layout and tidiness, but a tribute to German industry and determination, for their colony was created on drained swamps. They were ' employed' by the Turks in agriculture and in such useful ways as the building of the first paved road from Haifa to Nazareth and the Sea of Galilee.

The name Haifa, like that of Jaffa, means 'beautiful', though some have attempted to make Caiaphas, its founder, and say the name derives from him. The British Mandate developed the harbour and an oil pipe-line and Haifa became Palestine's second city. Later, Israel having created Tel Aviv, Haifa was made third city. Its development continues.

I have got caught up in history now. You might like to know that the name Carmel is a contraction of Karem-el, meaning 'the vineyards of Him (God)'. I don't remember seeing many vineyards and I should imagine there are now mainly houses where the vines once grew. One other place I remember on the lower slopes of Carmel that had some interest for us was the Military Staff College. From time to time, we got to know some of the officers training there and one became the husband of a colleague of mine. Her wedding reception was held in our school hall. A beautiful cake was made for her after much saving up of ingredients. Alas, it was found that the treasured butter had gone rancid; no fridges then, at best an ice-box. Just one of the very minor accidents of war!

By 1943, food problems were becoming more pressing. Those of us on the school staff who were younger would often go over the road to the foot of Carmel to a little sweet shop to get something to fill the corners. There was no real chocolate to be had, but there was something called 'chocolate'; that famous word 'ersatz' had entered the language. What we bought was 'ersatz' but eatable, probably made from the Carob tree, from locust beans. What more suitable than being sustained by the fruit that sustained John the Baptist near Ain Karim – quite unrecognisable to him of course, as his beans would be unrecognisable to most people eating World War Two chocolate concoctions.

Not far from the sweet shop and near the school was St. Luke's Church, where one of the Allinson brothers was Rector; his two brothers were also Middle East clergy and both became Bishops. Soon after I arrived, Roger married one of the staff from Christ Church, Jerusalem. We attended the church every Sunday. My most vivid memory of a service there is of a little girl, just able to talk, turning herself round in her chair and saying in her loud baby voice, "Do you like my new shoes?" In a whisper, I assured her they were very pretty (they were red ones) while smiles went round the congregation. Light relief like that did not often occur in church in those days.

That reminds me of going to a service on some festive occasion in a Greek Orthodox church. Most people were standing, with children sitting on the floor (ground, I think). Everyone had a candle. The service was rather long and small children were getting tired and hungry. I was not very happy to see that they took to peeling off the melted tallow that had run down the candles and popping it in their mouths!

One Arab member of our staff, Victoria Hakim, was often tempted away from her Greek Orthodox Church to ours. She liked the greater order and reverence, she said, of the Anglican Church. Later, she married and went to live in America. I have now heard that she has been very happy in her church and adopted country.

On one occasion, I was invited to a home where a new member of the family was to be baptised; house baptisms were the custom. I wrote home; "A week or two ago I went to the Christening of an Arab baby. His people belong to the Greek Orthodox Church and the Christening was held in the house. There were three priests and the baby was dipped right into the water (three times, I believe). As at all services of the Greek Orthodox Church, there was a great deal of moving about and talking and it was all very happy and homely. The next night I went to a party in honour of the son and heir and had a very nice time. We ate the most delicious Arab food. I want to learn how to make some Arab things before I come home."

Entry into local homes was always interesting. There was one visit, however, that I did not enjoy. The father of one of our girls died suddenly and it was thought fitting that some of the staff should pay a condolence call to her and her mother. As well as being sad, it was also difficult for them and I felt it so, too. It revealed one thing which we know, that some of our girls were the first generation of educated women in their families. This day, the mother sat on the floor in native dress while we were given bentwood chairs.

As in Jerusalem, I enjoyed plenty of hospitality from girls and their parents, Jewish and Arab, Christian and Moslem. I first drank mulled wine in a Jewish home, I visited an aristocratic Moslem home where a princely Sheikh was visiting and he tried to persuade me to become governess to one of his daughters. When I went back and told the Headmistress that I had the chance of joining an oriental royal household, she said "Don't consider it. You don't know what he would want next!" And that was that!

Sometimes, I had English invitations: one was to go sailing, another new experience; unfortunately my old propensity to travel sickness overcame me. I wrote home: "Of course, I was sea-sick, but I enjoyed it." The same kind gentleman included me in his 'crew' several times, but as I could never get out of the harbour decently, I at length thought that, even if I had not had enough (I badly wanted to sail in the beautiful crescent bay) he must have had enough of me. I think he understood when I declined to try again.

There were sometimes dinners out. Once or twice, a friend and I were invited to their Mess by two RNVR officers. At the end of the meal, they produced REAL chocolates. Unfortunately, I got a hard one and cracked a tooth. That led me to a good Jewish dental chair – all new experience is to be enjoyed! On another occasion, the cousin of a colleague was in Haifa with a friend. They wanted an evening out and my friend asked me to go with her. I was introduced to George and Tommy (names not quite accurate). They were both tall and handsome and well turned out by their batmen: You could almost see your face in their Sam Browns. A little later, she told me "You know Tommy is the Earl of --." I think it was his obituary I read a few months ago.

The same good lady soon after that married a widower; again the reception was in our hall. I wrote in a letter "There were about 60 guests. We had a busy time decorating the Church (a change from examinations and reports) and arranging everything, but we all enjoyed it." Sadly, she died of cancer before very long.

I have already told you of the wedding of Marion Gilmour and Dennis Small in Jerusalem. That took place in November, 1943. (I think I stayed at the American Hospice, but my husband – then the Best Man – thinks I stayed at the Scottish Hospice: a little domestic difference after 55 years!) Certainly, in 1944 I had another short holiday in Jerusalem, about September, and stayed in the Scottish hospice. I remember a slightly cussed elderly lady saying, "Which room have they given you? When I had replied, she retorted acerbicly, "That room! The sun shines in there day and night!" I wrote home about this visit: "Did I tell you what a nice time I had this holiday in Jerusalem? I did quite a number of things with Frank Gidney that I had not done before. We visited the big Jewish Hospital (the Hadassah) on the Mount of Olives one day and afterwards picniced on the hillside. The hospital is a wonderful one. Another day, we went to my beloved Ain Karim and in the evenings we heard concerts usually and one night went to a play and one night a cinema .... I had a very nice time." A Padre in the Hospice took us to various interesting services which I had not attended before." Frank soon had military duties elsewhere and was soon posted to Belgium, so that I could not see him again. We later met in the UK.

Now, dear reader (as they used to say), how would you have liked an expedition in your schooldays to Jericho and Jerusalem? I am going to tell you about the one I had with some of our Haifa girls during the Easter holidays in 1943. I shall be quoting almost an entire letter that I sent home. "I had eighteen girls from the top two senior classes and one Jewish Old Girl and one Arab teacher to help me. We hired our own bus. (Although I had sometimes travelled on ordinary service buses alone, with friends or a few girls, our numbers, our luggage and our desire to be without accompanying hens, lambs, surprise packages and all kinds of distractions made a private conveyance essential.)

Different modes of travel, seen on our way

We set out at 8 a.m. On our journey, we visited the ruins of Megiddo, passed through Nablus, saw Jacob's Well and then drove on to Ramallah, which is quite near Jerusalem. There we stayed in an Armenian Quaker school. All the girls slept in one very large dormitory, the other two helpers shared a room and I had a tiny one to myself. We arrived about 1 p.m. and sat down and ate the picnic lunch we had brought with us. We had intended to eat it on the way, but suddenly the weather had turned bitterly cold, too cold (and wet even) for out of door picnics.

After lunch, most of the girls rested, but a few of them came shopping with me. We had an early tea and then went to the Rural Training Centre in Ramallah, a Government place where village teachers are trained in handicrafts, poultry farming, cooking, etc. to go to teach in the villages. The girls enjoyed seeing the turkeys and models of all the costumes of Palestine and all sorts of other things, especially a bee that stung my leg! (Why did he choose me?) We had a delicious supper and later I gave them all cocoa in bed, which they greatly enjoyed.

Next day, we went to Jerusalem and walked round the city walls, visited the Garden of Gethsemane and its churches and saw the old city. In the afternoon, we went to Bethlehem. That night, Miss Sifri and I had supper with the Ramallah staff and the girls were left to themselves till bed-time. Just before bed, we sat in front of the fire and talked and they sang. Most of them sat on the floor while I, like a grandmother, had the rocking chair.

On the Wednesday, we went to Jericho and picniced by the Dead Sea. It was pleasantly warm, but not a bit too hot. In the afternoon, we had a tea party and finally in the evening, a supper party. After supper, we went to look at local embroideries and to everyone's delight I tried on a Ramallah dress.

Ramallah work (red thread on white background)

"Next day, Thursday, the last day, we went to a pottery, to the Museum and then to the Jerusalem Girls' College, where we picniced in the garden. We got back to Haifa about 7 p.m., having gathered oranges and grapefruit from trees on the way. We were all tired, but I think very happy. I now have a delightful little book which was made for me as a souvenir. It is very charmingly illustrated, quite one of my treasures in fact."

I had had some apprehension about going to Haifa and missing my Jerusalem girls, but this letter indicates that I was finding my work just as rewarding in Haifa. It continues:

> "Before school began, I had a week-end with a very nice Jewish family on the mountain (Carmel). They were very kind to me.[5]

At that time in Haifa, I wrote home, "Since term began, I've been very busy. I think I enjoy my work more than ever. Tell Auntie Lizzie it's not the girls that are turning my hair grey. I love them."

Sometimes, however, one could not help being saddened. I was teaching in a room that overlooked the harbour. Suddenly, there came a crash and a great commotion. Girls rushed to the window. I got them back in place and we read something, but I don't think anyone took much in. A refugee ship had arrived and the desperate people were not allowed to land. There was more than one occasion like this, lives were lost and survivors were sent to Cyprus. I did not like the political decision that brought about this suffering. The British Government was naturally blamed by the Jews; but if the Mandatory Power had allowed landing, the Arabs would have been casting the blame. That is all I can say in defence. (It is always difficult to be the one in the middle of two quarrelling parties). I resolved when I began; rosy spectacles, no politics.

From time to time, there were strikes by one side or the other and girls sometimes stayed away. On one occasion, I disagreed with the Headmistress when she blamed two or three Jewish girls who arrived late, not in uniform. I said they should have credit for coming; if in uniform they might have been mocked on their bus or even prevented from coming at all. I think she then saw my point. I did, however, tell a class that I disapproved of schoolgirls striking and, in answer to a question "Will they have to do their homework?" replied "Yes, they will." Someone, being somewhat argumentative, then said "But they are doing it for their country." I then smiled and tried to get a laugh by saying, "You both think it is your country, don't you? So it is – together. Let's just get on with our work and be happy together, as we all normally are." The lesson proceeded ...... But, of course, will the problem ever go away?

My teaching career took a new turn while I was in Haifa. I had my first experience of teaching boys. I did not find many classroom differences. The boys were perhaps less inclined to enjoy poetry, or to admit that they enjoyed it. I did not get to know any of the boys well, as I knew the girls. I did not see as much of them as I was only 'lent' for a few periods a week. I

---

[5] Footnote:2010: The schoolgirl of that visit still writes to me. Not many are now left to do that! Recently, she sent me a book of Carmel flowers – lovely in the 40's. Carmel is now very built up, she has told me.

used to walk from the girls' school to the boys' school, St. Lukes. (I may have taken a bus part of the way, or had a lift occasionally). I can remember running and jumping over rocky ground covered in low bushy plants, some with little pink flowers. I do not know their names. I enjoyed going to and fro. Once or twice, I stayed for a week-end at St. Luke's and I was invited there for part of a holiday. I knew three of their teachers quite well. Dennis Baly, Michael King and John Harrison had all worked at the boys' school in Jerusalem, St. George's, and so I had met them there. Dennis Baly I had known slightly at Liverpool, where his father was a Professor of Chemistry. Dennis had taken a geography degree and had begun his teaching career at the Bishop's School in Amman. In 1939, he moved to St. George's School, Jerusalem, as Housemaster: from there, after two years he moved to St. Luke's School, Haifa. He remained there till the school closed in 1948. Later, he tried to get the school re-opened, but the Jewish authorities would not give permission. St. George's School was surviving, however, and Dennis became joint Headmaster there with an Armenian. I learnt later that Dennis had gone to America, married and become a Professor and an authority on the geography of the Holy Land, with a number of books to his name. Sadly, in 1987, he was killed in an accident.

Of John Harrison and Michael King I know less. I enjoyed knowing them as well as Dennis and also Doris Robinson, on the Haifa Boys' School staff while I was there. John Harrison married and took Holy Orders. Michael King, who had intended to enter the Church after the war, did not do so, but did noble work for refugees and with the World Council of Churches. Doris I got to know well and we kept in touch after we both returned home. She had an Oxford History degree and eventually took up Training College work. She was a woman of great courage, very disabled with both legs in calipers. Nothing daunted her and she had a great sense of humour.

One of my underlying themes in writing this 'memoir' has been to show how different a teaching life abroad could be from one at home. What little things come to mind before leaving Haifa? At one time, there was a plague scare which led to a great anti-rat campaign. I remember a girl reporting that she had seen a dead rat on her way to school. The Headmistress lost no time in contacting the authorities and ensuring its immediate removal. I remember too, the firm reply to a girl who complained of bites acquired (at school, I believe). The Headmistress asked if the biter was a bug; the girl shuddered and said she did not know what a bug looked like. "Then, in this country and this hot weather, that is knowledge you should certainly have." I felt a certain sense of shared guilt; I am glad to say I have never yet acquired that knowledge.

The Headmistress was not without a sense of humour. She recounted one day how she had had a telephone call from an official who said, "I know you are a very "CONSCIENCE" lady, so I am offering you some cracked eggs." (Local English was not always quite right! Eggs were by then severely rationed, so the cracked ones were accepted with alacrity and, with the pig 'bubble' then prevailing, we were able to enjoy bacon and eggs for breakfast.

I told you about Jerusalem food; a word or two more about diet in Haifa. Catering had become more difficult, but we always fed quite adequately. We each had our own tin of sugar. In our garden, there were pomegranates and masses of nasturtiums; I thought the pomegranates very beautiful but disappointing to eat; instead of lettuce we ate constant nasturtium leaves in sandwiches and salads. Oranges abounded as they had done in Jerusalem. One saw mountains of them piled up outside the Damascus Gate in Jerusalem. At one time, I wrote home: "We have so many oranges in Palestine, rotting on the trees, being burnt by the roadside, or being sold for a song; what a pity you can't have a few." I never like sharp, acid fruit and could not understand why, in Haifa day after day, we had green oranges that I found it difficult to eat.

To conclude on food: I was taken very much by surprise at the end of the war when the Headmistress, flying home for some leave, said, "I'm going to ask you to take over the housekeeping." Our cook was a real old retainer who, we younger staff thought, relieved the Headmistress of decisions on food by just giving us over-frequently the things she liked cooking, some of which we did not like at all. I had first to win the confidence and good-will of 'Cookie' (she was really a nice, ample, good-hearted, fairly elderly Arab) and then I increased my popularity with my colleagues by varying the menus considerably.

Having mentioned our cook, I must not forget our henchman. He was a noble figure in white galabieh and red tarbush. After breakfast, he always came into the dining room and we could each tell him if we wanted him to bring anything for us from the town. I was astonished on being told that he could not read or write, but had the most amazing memory. His notebook was just the mark of his office. Perhaps we don't exercise our memories enough. Muslims learn the Koran by heart and learning by heart seems to come naturally to many Arabs. We should not despise learning by rote (especially the memorising of poetry). I could say a lot more on different ways of learning and becoming 'educated', but I said at the beginning that I was not going to attempt a treatise on teaching techniques. So here I stop.

21. Holidays from Haifa

Cyprus

For shorter holidays while in Haifa, I usually returned to Jerusalem. Once I went to Damascus. I think I have told you of this already, the not so successful time when I had sandfly fever. The most interesting holidays I had during 1943-5 were in Cyprus, which I visited two or three times, and Egypt where I spent my last holiday, a very short one.

I write of these two places with some heartache, for then, against a backdrop of World War, they seemed peaceful and friendly. Now, as I write, the great sites of Egypt are deserted, the desert deserted, because tourists have been massacred by fanatical Moslems, much against the wishes of the equally Moslem, but tolerant Egyptian government.

In Cyprus too, I was reminded in the paper this morning of the 'Green Line' that divides the Moslem ruled Turkish north from the Greek Christian south, so that beautiful island likewise cannot offer that deep sense of peace that holidays at best, holy-days, gave me on my visits in the early 1940's.

Cyprus is a lovely island. Not being divided when I was there, we could move round freely from place to place. The first area I visited was Paphos, which had been a place of pilgrimage in the ancient world. It was a centre of Hellenistic culture and celebrated as the birthplace of Aphrodite, who rose from the waves on its shores. The coastline here is very craggy, not

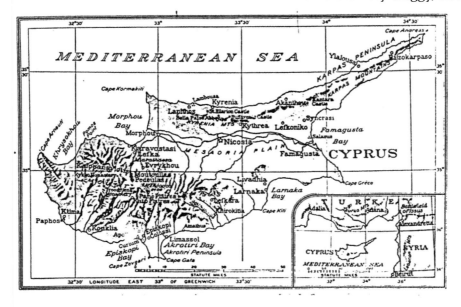

inviting for bathing. Did Aphrodite have to scramble ashore over the toe-piercing rocks or was it a softer shore in those days? Perhaps earthquakes have affected it. Once over the rocks, the land beyond was probably even then more hospitable. Now there are steeply terraced vineyards and on the slopes of the Troodos mountains, thick pine forests. The moist west winds from the sea are warm, the rainfall is good and tropical fruits can be grown.

In the 1940's, Paphos seemed an almost deserted place; the friend I was travelling with, an historian, acted as my guide. There were no tourists anywhere and not a soul at the sites associated with Aphrodite or St. Paul. Paul and Barnabas reached Paphos in 47 AD and converted the Roman Pro-Consul to Christianity. This must have made Cyprus the first Christian ruled area in the Ancient World. In the 4th century BC, it had been ruled by the Ptolemies of Egypt. In the 2nd century BC Paphos became its capital and remained so after the Romans arrived in 58 BC until it was finally destroyed by earthquakes, of which there were many till the 4th century AD, when Salamis succeeded Paphos as capital with the name of Constantia.

To be honest, I remember very little of what I saw in Paphos. The sites now restored and looked after and attracting tourists were then neglected; here and there a few columns, piles of stones, half grassed over, perhaps some sheltering trees. Here, Aphrodite was worshipped; there possibly St. Paul stood. One felt the past; now I would love to return to see more historic evidence and, especially, mosaics. Churches, half ruined, neglected, restored and monasteries used and unused, are everywhere a part of the Cyprus scene. Often, amid stately cypresses and other trees, they add greatly to the beauty of the country.

In the Paphos area, there are the remains of a larger church, originally of the 4th century. It is the Khrysolplitissa basilica. It is one I would seek out if I could return to Cyprus. By contrast, I might visit the district Ayios Georgyious and see the 6th century mosaics of a church dedicated to St. George with a Byzantine chapel and a new church honouring England's patron saint. Here, St. George's main patronage seems to be to lovers and shepherds, his military origin being quite forgotten. Perhaps love pervades the area, for I believe the spot where Aphrodite is said to have stepped ashore is not far away.

If you are going to Cyprus, I recommend a quick look at Salamis. In Paphos, we thought mainly of Paul, but in Salamis, our thoughts are turned to his companion, Barnabas. There is a monastery dedicated to St. Barnabas, who was born here, then brought up in Jerusalem, returned with Paul and Mark, converted many: eventually he was martyred at the stake in his native city. He is patron saint of the Cypriot Orthodox Church. The local archbishop enjoys special privileges, one of which is to sign his name in purple ink. The monastery, although a 5th century foundation, is an 18th century building.

Visit Cyprus in Springtime to see its wild flowers. The Roman ruins of Salamis, with some great carved columns, have much of the magic of ruins, as they soar above a carpet of golden petals, perhaps with a half revealed mosaic beneath them.

A Typical Cyprus church. This stands on the site of the Synagogue in Paphos where St. Paul preached.

When the Arabs sacked Salamis c.700, many people left and settled in Famagusta. Armenians were forcibly settled in Famagusta in the 12th century. In the 13th century, Acre, the last crusader stronghold, fell to the 'infidels' and more refugees came to Cyprus. Thanks to its central situation and the Pope's stern command of no trading with the infidels in Palestine, and to hard work by the fresh-start population, Famagusta flourished. It was said that, at evening feasts, the tables were laden not only with food, but with flowers, and jewels to be taken away as gifts. Riches bring envy and Genoese and Venetians came to get rich. Eventually, the Venetians took over, but their ruler was mercilessly tricked by the Ottomans, who established a long rule. One of my few memories of Famagusta is the cathedral of St. Nicholas, turned mosque. Church conversion was frequent: better than complete destruction? Yes, I think on the whole: the conclusion I came to in Hagia Sophia in Istanbul. Strange things have become of churches in our own land, but another church in Famagusta has 'served the community' in a strange medley of ways – mosque, potato store (under the British!) and moving upwards has now become the Town Hall.

Nicosia, the capital of Cyprus, is a divided city today, but it is capital on both sides of the Green Line, the dividing line. It was not divided when I visited it briefly. I remember little of it, but I saw Saint Sophia Cathedral, built in the 13th century in French Gothic style and made into the Selimya Mosque at the time of the Ottoman Conquest. Minarets were added in 1570 to replace the steeples. On these conversions, I have already commented.

I was also in Kyrenia briefly. I think I was there with Margaret Ashe and one of my Arab colleagues, Samera Haddad. I have a photograph of the three of us standing near the north-east tip of that narrow strip of land that stretches out to sea like a long pointing finger. We must have got there from Kyrenia – on foot! I remember saying years afterwards when asked where were the most beautiful places I had seen that this point in Cyprus was the nearest to a fairy-tale. Where we stood we looked back to a castle, half-ruined and more romantic in its broken form than it would have been in newness. In the other direction was the final point of land and a tiny island beyond in the bluest of blue shaded turquoise to peacock Mediterranean sea. The land we stood on was emerald grass and golden rocks. One could not live there but the memory lives forever.

The three of us!

Two places to visit from Kyrenia are the fortress, church, palace remains of St. Hilarion and Bellapais Abbey in what is now known as Lawrence Durrell country. Read his "Bitter Lemons".

Twice, we stayed at Makhlouf's Camp in the Troodos area. It was usually referred to as a hotel camp. We each had a bedroom tent and there was a large dining tent and a marquee for socialising, which served as a refuge if rain came. One felt very close to nature.

Makhlouf's Camp

The approach to Troodos was a long twisting climb by car through Platres and other beautiful mountainside suburbs with English style houses, one of them being mansion-size and the Governor's summer residence, later taken over to be the Greek President's summer home. Roads were tree-shaded and the houses one passed had beautiful gardens.

On the mountain there were many pleasant walks. The dominant tree was the Aleppo Pine, but there were some cedars. In Cedar Valley, there were magnificent specimens claimed to surpass the cedars of Lebanon. My artist friend and companion made a painting for me here, which is reproduced below.

Troodos, Cyprus.

I remember visiting a village from our mountain fastness, where I bought sponges, long since gone, and embroidered table mats now used more as sentimental memories than for dinner parties!

I think I have already said there are innumerable monasteries in Cyprus. I remember visiting one. It was such a tortuous climb to reach it that I thought I must be going to my heavenly mansion somewhere in the shadow. When I got there, I saw heavenly icons but once more monks were employed in the homely making of bread, a reminder that I had not yet reached heaven. The descent increased my travel sickness, so that I felt horribly terrestrial till the next day. The most famous monastery in the island is Kykko. The name seems familiar, but I cannot honestly identify it as the one I visited.

Egypt

My last middle-eastern holiday, and a very short one, was to Egypt. Egypt in a week! Just a little more. My Head Mistress encouraged me not to miss it and I remain grateful for her help. Catherine Lacey, a somewhat older colleague who remained my lasting friend, came with me. We travelled by train at Easter time – or was it Christmas? The weather was ideal for us, although a little hot: friends who had gone on honeymoon at Christmas time had snow there! So I think it was Easter when we went. Gertrude Bell and her party must have gone in winter, judging by their clothes, which seem surprising.

Gertrude Bell in 1921, with Winston Churchill on her right and
T E Lawrence on her left. (Note the clothes in which they rode!)

At university, I had got to know a number of Egyptian students studying there and we had sought the points at which Moslems and Christians could come together in friendship and understanding. There were other little jerks towards Egypt from time to time, so there was a sense of fulfilment in getting there at last. I want to begin my miniature of Egypt with a look at an Egyptian garden. There are no human fences in gardening; gardens and gardeners everywhere understand each other. Their weapons are only shears for discreet pruning. By the Temple of Hatshepsut, where murder was recently enacted Hatshepsut had created beautiful terraced gardens. There may be desert there now, but it was not always so. Hatshepsut had gardener predecessors. It seems there was a long tradition of gardening in Ancient Egypt. Ordinary gardeners like us lived there thousands of years ago. I cannot remember where I found this quotation, but I hope it will delight you as it delighted me. A poem of 1900 BC. I am sorry it has to be in translation! Hieroglyphics are beyond me!!

> ### *Tale of the Garden Flowers*
> *"She led me, hand in hand, and we went into her garden to*
> *   converse together.*
> *There she made me taste of excellent honey.*
> *The rushes of the garden were verdant and all its bushes*
> *   flourishing.*
> *There were currant trees and cherries redder than ruby:*
> *The ripe peaches of the garden resembled bronze*
> *And the groves and the lustre of the stone 'rashem'.*
> *The 'menni' unshelled like cocoa-nuts they brought to us*
> *The shade was fresh and airy and soft for the repose of*
> *   love,*
> *The garden is today in its glory*
> *There is a terrace and a parlour."*

Our Elizabethan gardens had arbour's provision for love also. Here is an Egyptian love-lyric:

> *"Come through the garden, Love, to me*
> *My love is like each flower that blows*
> *Tall and straight as a young palm-tree*
> *And in each cheek a sweet blush-rose."*

Now we move on to 1100 BC. Here are the words of the great King of Assyria, Tiglath-Pileser, one-time conqueror of Egypt, who wrote:

> *"Cedars and box and allakanu wood have I carried off from the*
> *countries I conquered, trees that none of my forefathers have pos-*

sessed; these trees have I taken, and planted them in mine own coun-
try, in the parks of Assyria have I planted them."

Our first day in Egypt I think we did what most tourists do, we made for the Sphinx and the Pyramids at Giza. The Sphinx, a figure with a lion's body and a man's face, a possible portrait of a Pharoah, perhaps Khephren of the third pyramid, has a perpetual fascination; it presents an enigma, the inscrutable, the eternal riddle. Now the riddle seems to be how to pre-serve the crumbling stone. One man slept at the foot of the Sphinx and had a dream that if he cleaned up the surroundings of the monuments, he would become Pharaoh. He went to work without delay and did indeed become Pharaoh! – so the story says. Egypt had three great periods in her ancient history: the Old Kingdom, 3998-3335 BC, the Middle Kingdom, 3005-2112 BC and the New Kingdom, 1738-1102 BC. There are intermediate periods and later ones. Then comes mainly foreign domination; Persian, Ptolemaic, Roman and Arab.

Frank and his brother, John, waiting for a prophecy from the Sphinx!

The Sphinx belongs to the Middle Kingdom. There are other sphinxes to be seen and earlier ones did not have the human portrait head, but a falcon or a ram's head. An avenue of ram-headed sphinxes leads into Karnak.

The pyramids are not far from the Sphinx, indeed the leading ones form its background. Of the wonders of the ancient world, the pyramids are the only one still standing. For a long time they were the highest buildings in the world. Cologne Cathedral was the first building to exceed them; I sup-pose many more buildings are higher now.

I see the pyramids as standing aloof in a rocky desert sandscape, but the Giza district encroaches more and more on their privacy and sometimes the flooding Nile is near. I wonder if the Egyptians still use the name Pyramid Road for the main road in the area. It was built at the time of the opening of the Suez Canal; the French engineer De Lesseps was honoured and Napoleon III and Empress Eugenie made a royal progress to visit the pyramids. Incidentally, I know that, also to celebrate the opening of the Suez Canal, Verdi's "Aida" was performed in the Ezbekiah Gardens: every lady attending was given a programme which entitled her to one share in the Suez Canal. This was the gift of Prince Mohammad Ali Pasha.

The pyramids of Giza were built at the beginning of the Old Kingdom in the 4th Dynasty, one of the great periods of Egyptian history. There are nine pyramids in all, three of kings and six of the queens of two of them.

The Pyramids at Giza

The three kings are Khufu, Menkauri and Khephren (Greek historians turned these names into Cheops, Mykerenos and Chefren). It seems that Khufu and Khephren disagreed with the priests, regarding them as corrupt and imposing heavy taxes related to temple sacrifices. Khufu closed the temples and was loved by the people, according to one account. He employed men to work on his pyramid only while the Nile was in flood and they could not work their land. They were glad to be fed and housed by him. The opposite view says that he harassed the men and they worked for 10 years making a road and 20 years on the pyramid. One has heard how slaves were forced to build the pyramids, no one knowing exactly how the heavy stones were brought to the site and erected, though it is fairly certain that ramps were used to raise them. The modern view seems to be more in keeping with the kindlier view of Khufu.

The Khufu pyramid is the largest ever built. The stone was probably brought from all over Egypt. It was originally 480 feet high, but Saladin took some stones to build a palace and others have removed a few. When I was there, one or two people were climbing up it. I was tempted to try a few steps myself: no one there to stop us. It was too hard a task for me and not fun at all really. Anyway, I thought more stones would only be worn away by too many climbers! My friend suggested a camel ride instead, so I mounted a camel (a dizzy experience) admiring its carpet saddle and soon I decided that it was also carpeted underfoot. It padded along as if in carpet slippers. I was glad it did not try gargling while I was on its back. You may remember that gargling had been recommended to me as a way or pronouncing certain Arabic sounds. I enjoyed my ride, but give me the humble donkey in preference to the lofty camel. (More about camels in Things That do not Change).

A 19th century lady was more daring and determined than I about climbing the pyramid of Khufu or Cheops. I quote from her own account of her adventure. She was carried over the Nile by two Egyptians. She says: "This was one of the most disagreeable things that can be imagined. Two large powerful men stood side by side; I mounted on their shoulders and, held fast by their heads while they supported my feet above the waters, which in some places reached almost to their armpits, so that I feared every moment that I should sit in the water." Her crossing in 1852 lasted about a quarter of an hour. I do not think mine lasted as long as that on the little ferry boat in 1944.

We sometimes think of Victorian females as feeble and given to fainting and vapours, but when they had a sense of adventure, you might say that they stopped at nothing. One lady, Ida Pfeiffer, had her rings removed before making her climb, because the fellows who assisted pyramid climbers had "such a dextrous knack of drawing the rings from fingers" that the owners "seldom perceive their loss until too late." The climb was arduous and lasted about three quarters of an hour. "Two Arabs ascended first," she says "and then stretched out their hands to pull me from one block to another. I preferred climbing over the smaller blocks without assistance."

When she had gained the summit, she was stunned by the thought that she was "one of the favoured few able to contemplate the most stupendous and imperishable monument ever erected by human hands." She saw below her the Nile flowing and a few Bedouin looking like pygmies. She ceased to wonder that the pyramids are reckoned among the seven wonders of the world. As they are indeed the only surviving wonder of the original seven, perhaps I should have made the climb!

The modern entrance to the pyramid is one made by robbers. The walls of their tunnel are rough; the original walls smoothly faced. There are several sarcophagus chambers, one a Great Gallery. I did not enjoy penetrating the gloomy interior of the pyramid and we had no desire to enter either of the others. The Kephren pyramid appears to be the highest, but this is only because it has kept more of its facing stones. Menkauri's sarcophagus within, we were told, is more highly decorated than the others, but we were not induced to see for ourselves. The priests of his day preferred him to Khufu and Khepren because he favoured them and reopened the temples.

The Giza pyramids are by no means the only ones in Egypt. We visited Sakkara and saw the step pyramids. Sakkara is the burial ground for the ancient capital of Memphis, not my favourite sort of place. Memphis was once the capital of all Egypt. It also seems to have been a vast burial ground. After being capital of Lower Egypt, situated as it is centrally, it was the obvious capital of the united country. It was a cosmopolitan metropolis. There was an ancient belief that whoever held Memphis would rule the country. This, and financial prosperity, lured many nationalities to settle within its boundaries, among them Libyans, Phoenicians, Jews, Persians, Armenians and Greeks.

Tutankamun had a royal residence here and where the Pharaoh dwelt there was the capital. Other kings also made it their capital, leaving Thebes, the great ancient capital in Upper Egypt.

To Thebes we went the next day. Thebes originally in pharaonic times was situated on the east and west sides of the Nile. In modern times, the name is used for the West Bank only, with its burial grounds; on the East Bank are the great temples of Karnak and Luxor – and the leading hotels. I think we stayed most of the time in the Winter Palace overlooking the Nile, although I seem to have been in the Mena House part of the time. We watched the feluccas on the river and the sunsets of oriental splendour.

Ancient Egypt is overwhelming. The temples are colossal. The engineering, architectural and labouring skills stagger one's powers of comprehension and imagination. The historical and religious background demands a life-time's study. It is all fascinating, often beautiful. One is glad to have glimpsed it and sometimes in my dream-world, I have again been wandering among the colossal walls and towering lotus-headed pillars, trying to weave my way through dynasties and religious rites. Depicted on the walls, one can see the rite of the birth of a pharaoh and a festival procession from Karnak to Luxor at the time of the rising of the Nile.

In a dream, you come face to face with huge statues; some with attendant figures, a wife or daughter tucked in between the huge legs of someone like Rameses II or Amenophis III or Thuthmosis III; even the names are overpowering and yet all these people had all the human passions, including rivalries, jealousies and pride. It seems to have been the custom for the kings to tell of their own great deeds (often military). They write of 'My Majesty' – arrogance to us, but remember the Pharaoh was acknowledged as a god moving among gods.

Luxor

Visit Luxor first. It will acclimatise you to the vastness which is even greater at Karnak. Luxor was 'subordinate' to Karnak and linked to it by an avenue of sphinxes, some of whom remain. We were driven along the avenue in a kind of barouche, a gharry. It seemed like a royal progress, since we were living in the world of kings. Nectamebo I had erected these sphinxes, all of them identical portrait sphinxes – whose portrait? I suspect Nectamebo's – quite a good looking, though stony countenance.

I cannot remember when, where or how, but at some point after a break from the 'photographic or photogenic' sphinxes, we found ourselves (now walking, I think) along an avenue of ram-headed sphinxes, approaching walls that seemed hundreds of times taller than we were.

The Avenue of Ram-Headed Sphinxes at Karnak

As in Luxor, the temple was 'dedicated' (if that is the word) to Amun, to Khons and to Mut. Within, on the walls, we soon noticed reliefs of boats – Amun's bearing a ram, Khon's a falcon and Mut's, since she was a mother-god, showed a woman's head. The king (Rameses III, I believe) was shown sacrificing to the gods. The gods and the pharaohs – alive and dead – made good use of boats. On the shores of the Nile one understood why: a trip along the river from Luxor to Karnak would be relatively cool and pleasant and boats were needed to cross the Nile. The great God of the Sun was believed to sail across the sky and back every day, thus giving dawn and dusk, day and night. On the walls of tombs, boats are provided for the great journey and for lesser ones of life and death.

Rameses II had quite a lot to do with Karnak. Just outside the walls stand two huge statues of him, made of pink granite. He and his father were probably responsible for the great colonnaded hall into which we soon move. It is immense, with a central aisle for processions, and side aisles, the walls inscribed and decorated. Some of the roof remains and many of the enormous pillars, some painted, that held it up. The pillars, especially the capitals, in Egyptian architecture interested me. (Did the Greek and Roman Doric, Ionic, Corinthian ideas come from Egypt?) Papyrus and lotus provided the inspiration and then the tradition. To me, having experienced palm-leaf and bamboo buildings in Borneo, it is interesting to think of papyrus and mud-clay structures when visiting the great, sophisticated temples of Egypt. Wattle and daub, or equivalent, often provided more substantial buildings. Egyptian pillars go back to bundles of papyrus. The mop head of the papyrus was not suitable for a capital, so the lotus was brought in to fulfil the needs. Symbolically, they represented the United Kingdom, the papyrus being the emblem of Lower Egypt and the lotus the emblem of Upper Egypt. A papyrus pillar has a stranded effect – rushes bound together. The capitals may be lotus-bud (from the blue lotus), rose lotus, palm leaf, flower or foliage or some are Hathor headed – multiple heads of the wife of Horus.

In the temple of Karnak, there is so much to see that one ought to visit it many times. Inscribed or incised on pillars and walls one can see much history recorded, especially the conquests of the Pharaohs. Their defeated enemies are often portrayed as cringing or being cruelly punished. But there are other things to see. There are the remains of a mosque and of a church, all within the temple complex; there is a Botanical Room, created by Tuthmosis III after his successful campaign in Syria. In the Bible, we are reminded that warrior monarchs brought back plants and trees to establish in their own countries: Tuthmosis'spoils were both plants and animals. He succeeded in naturalising some of them in Egypt, including the hen. Unfortunately, only parts of his plants survive; the walls illustrating them are broken.

I have coped with strange names in Palestine and in Borneo, but the names of all the Egyptian kings defeat me. In a lifetime, one really gets to know only a very few people. I think there are only three monarchs of Egypt whom I wish I could know better; they are Rameses II, Tutankhamun and Queen Hapshephsut. To pursue them, I have to cross the Nile.

Feluccas sail along the timeless Nile

I am now going to take the little Nile ferry that the locals use and go over from East Thebes to West Thebes. As soon as one steps on to the little landing stage on the west bank, one walks a few yards and sees the great Colossi of Memnon. They have fascinated people for centuries. Hewn from a single block of quartzite, these two huge seated figures were once situated outside a mortuary temple. The statues bear on their sides symbols of the unified Egypt. Two gods of the Nile are represented, knotting together the lotus and papyrus.

Memnon's mother was Eos, the Greek goddess of the dawn. For many centuries, one statue uttered a dawn song to his mother. It is thought that a crack was made in the statue during an earthquake in 27 BC. This caused temperature changes to produce the sound. Unromantically, the singing ended when the crack was repaired. A happy ending was engineered, however; the crack partially reopened, I presume. I went up to Memnon and was able to imagine that he gave me a sweet-sounding whisper. I was told to come at dawn and then I might hear the full sound of his singing. Now I am often awake at dawn, but then I could not rouse myself so early; anyway, who would take me across the ferry?

Soon after Memnon, we passed by the Ramessium. Once a statue of Ramesis II, sixty feet high, stood outside his palace there. We did not go into his mortuary temple, but there were signs of ruins and broken statues round about, some interesting: a huge one lay on the ground. It brought to mind one of my youthful links with Egypt, Shelley's poem, "Ozymandias of

Egypt". I had exactly the feeling which he expressed with such sensitivity and perception; one feels he had seen the fallen pharaoh, whether he had or not. Somewhere, sometime, I read that Ozymandias had been identified as Rameses II. I can't find that statement now.

Ozymandias

I met a traveller from an antique land
Who said: 'Two vast and trunkless legs of stone
Stand in the desert. Near them on the sand,
Half sunk, a shatter'd visage, lies whose frown
And wrinkled lip and sneer of cold command
Tell that its sculptor well those passions read
Which yet survive, stamp'd on these lifeless things,
The hand that mock'd them and the heart that fed;
And on the pedestal these words appear:
"My name is Ozymandias, king of kings:
Look on my works, ye Mighty, and despair!"
Nothing beside remains. Round the decay
Of that colossal wreck, boundless and bare,
The lone and level sands stretch far away.'
   Percy Bysshe Shelley

The Temple of Hatshepsut

After a passing glance at Rameses II, we went to the terrace temple of Queen Hatshepsut, the façade of which would do justice to any period in history. Out of the desert sand it rises into the cliff side. Hatshepsut was a woman to be reckoned with. In his declining years, her father, Thothmes I had made her co-regent in power with himself. Thothmes II reigned, somewhat weakly, for 13 years. Thothmes III was only a boy when he succeeded and then Hatshepsut seized her opportunity to claim full power. She made herself KING. It is said that some statues of her show her as almost male, even with a beard added, (false beards were worn by Pharaohs) but in others she is a beautiful strong woman. She was certainly strong. Her reign was peaceful and trade and the arts flourished. Her interest in architecture is shown in her temple in the valley called Deir el Bahri. It is beautiful and bears interesting inscriptions. One significant description attempts to prove her divine and of royal birth and hence her claim to the throne; another shows a trade expedition to the Land of Punt.

The galleys of the time are depicted floating down the Nile and the fishes are familiar, then strange fish appear belonging to the Red Sea. Was there then a waterway link between the two? it has been asked. Clearly, the ships got to Punt, where houses were built on piles over swampy land (I have seen such in Borneo, an early form of domestic architecture). The people of Punt appear not unlike the Egyptians but wearing a different kind of aproned dress.

A Galleon of Ancient Egypt

This great trading expedition was heavenly inspired, claimed Hatshepsut. One day, when at prayer in the Temple of Amen, she said that "a command was heard in the sanctuary, a behest of the god himself, that the ways that lead to Punt should be explored and that the roads that lead to the Ladders of Incense should be trodden."

Hatshepsut sent Parihu, the ruler of Punt, necklaces, bracelets and weapons and glass beads which were bartered, if not treasured. Pariku's wife, with her daughter, came down to greet the Egyptians. She was a very large lady; everyone was eager to be involved except, I imagine, the donkey that had to bring her.

The explorers and trading ambassadors, with their soldier guard, returned with a cargo greater than the one they had brought; gold, ebony, ivory, leopard skins, greyhounds, apes that frolicked over the galley and, best of all, incense gum or frankincense trees, with their root balls protected in baskets. They also managed to get a giraffe into the galley!

Queen Hatshepsut was especially overjoyed with her bowl of incense and had the beads of gum weighed out with a gold and silver measure and stored in the Temple. The frankincense trees she had planted on the terraces behind the Temples, calling it a "Paradise for Amen". She was a great gardener.

The populace gave the returning company a welcome such as that now given to triumphant footballers. Only the poor lonely giraffe, I imagine, failed to enjoy himself, as the crowd shouted and laughed at an animal stranger than any they had ever seen before.

Trade flourished under Hatshepsut. She enjoyed her successes and wrote about them and celebrated them. She wrote: "I was sitting in the palace and thinking of my Creator when my heart urged me to make for him in the hall of Columns two obelisks whose points should reach the sky." Her obelisks have survived much longer than her or her god.

When she died, she was not buried among the Queens, but in the Valley of the *Kings*, for it was as King she had determinedly lived her life – an ancient feminist, I think.

Hatshepsut's Obelisks

Are the obelisks still now on the banks of the Thames?

Tutankhamun

A Portrait
And we walked in a magical garden
With rivers and bowers
And my bed was of ivory and gold:
And the Queen breathed soft in my ear
A song of enchantment
And I never grew old...

Walter de la Mare

When I was about seven years old, Howard Carter discovered Tutankha-mun's tomb. It was headline news in all the papers (where we now all too often see murderers or other criminals, or sleazy figures on the front page, there was the golden young king.)

I don't know whether all children were told about it, but in my little private school our delightful teacher, Daphne Barber, caught our imaginations through her own enthusiasm for the finds. Whether she sowed the seeds of any future Egyptologists I do not know, but I think she may have been respon-sible for my desire to travel and see for myself. Incidentally, she confirmed that desire a little later: sadly she had left us and gone to India as governess to the little daughter of some high official. She sent me my first postcard from abroad, a picture of sunrise (or sunset?) over the Taj Mahal. I said to my mother, "Can we go and see it?" She replied, "It is too far away; but *you* might go there one day." I have never been. But I have seen Tutankhamun's tomb and some of his treasures in the Cairo Museum.

Was Miss Barber responsible for my curiosity and love of travel? – espe-cially among ruins!

There is a lot of suspense about Egypt. Howard Carter had worked in the Valley of the Kings for six full seasons in the hope of finding Tutan-kahmun's tomb, along with his patron, Lord Carnarvon; he was just packing up to leave, once more disappointed, when a deep cut in the soil was discovered below a workman's hut they were dismantling. Excitement and suspense became intense as they discovered stairs deep into the earth and then broke the seal on entrance after entrance until they finally found a jumble of possessions. The exhilaration of discovery and the fever of suspense had been almost unbearable when in the outer chambers they had found signs of earlier opening and plundering and then at last "A roomful – a whole museum full it seemed – of objects piled one upon another in seemingly endless profusion." I am quoting from Carter's own account. In this chaos there were:

"Three great gilt couches, their sides carved in the form of mon-strous animals, their heads throwing grotesque distorted shadows on the walls ... Two life-sized figures of a king in black facing each other like sentinels, gold kilted, gold sandaled, armed with mace and staff, the protective sacred cobra upon their foreheads. Piled one upon an-other there was a profusion of priceless objects, painted and inlaid caskets, bouquets of flowers, alabaster perfume vases, beds, chairs ... a pair of gilt sistra, an alabaster wishing cup ... A confusion of dismem-bered chariots glistening with gold." Carter's first impression as he began to see in the light of a flickering candle was one of gold – "eve-rywhere the glint of gold."

The Valley of the Kings, where the Royal Tombs are located

Most of these things I later saw in the Cairo Museum. I believe that during the war the museum was closed, at least for a time, and a special permit was needed to visit it. Somehow, I got in. Memory says I was quite alone when I was admitted to a scene which was more like a store-room or over-filled attic than a museum display. Like a commissionaire or security officer, a black and gold figure (one, not two) was guarding the entry, on sentry duty, a sentinel. It took me some time to realise that it was young

Tutankhamun himself – Was he acting a part, in youthful joking mood? Carter said the Egyptians were jolly people. I could have shaken hands with him. There was no one to say 'hands off', no notice 'Please do not touch!' I didn't touch, everything seemed too dusty and yet too sanctified or too precariously placed on top of something else. Was it all really meant to look just as Carter had found it? A new type of display? Nothing was labelled, no glass cases, no guardian barriers.

There was a golden bed, a chair, a fan and many of the things Carter mentioned – and I was alone with them all!

Things were not just as Carter had found them, because more had been found in the next chamber. My sentinel had a duplicate and, as Carter wondered where was the king's sarcophagus, he noticed that the two identical figures were guarding another 'doorway'. This had to be unsealed and then he found greater confusion than in the first; all the disorder he attributed to plunderers, who for some reason, had never come back to take their spoils.

Carter said the second chamber 'defied description'. Not a single inch of floor space remained empty. "It was a matter of extreme difficulty to move one object without running serious risk of damaging others." Altogether, much jewellery was found; rings, collars, necklaces, bracelets fashioned in gold with lapis lazuli, that favourite blue colour, and precious jewels. There was a beautiful pink ostrich feather fan, beaded slippers that had to be treated with wax to prevent them crumbling to a handful of beads; modern looking furniture, a golden boat, an inlaid cabinet, caskets, a child's chair (that little Tut probably used) and the exquisite chair,

Security Officer – one of those Carter "rescued"

the Throne that became the centre of my interest in the museum. Although it was not placed as a centre piece; it was just surrounded by all sorts of other things, nevertheless the dignified stylised figures of the King and his Queen depicted on the back <u>demanded</u> attention. In the decoration, Tutankahmun sits on a beautiful blue and gold chair in a relaxed position, while Ankheseamun, wearing the royal head-dress, anoints him gently from a golden box. Garments are beautifully pleated in a dark muted turquoise colour. (Very early Egyptians did not use pleats). Anointing is an age-old custom, religious anointing, royal anointing, the anointing of guests in welcome, the anointing of healing, the anointing of love. Clearly, the Queen is anointing in love, possibly also medicinally. Was she treating an ailing husband? We do not know why Tutanhamun died young. He was only eighteen it is said, having ruled since he was nine.

Religion was an important part of Egyptian life. Local gods were worshipped, originally animals, but later represented as humans with animal heads. Bast, the cat god, became one worshipped beyond her local district and very popular. Osiris was the god of resurrection and the after-life. Isis, his wife, was the mother god. Horus, then Re, the sun god, was the god of the good life in this world. He was essentially Pharaoh's god and Pharaoh was himself a god, always considered the offspring of Re.

Tutankhamun being anointed with oil by his young Queen, Ankhesenamun

Tutankhamun's predecessor, Akhenaten, had tried to change the complicated systems of deities, reduce the multifarious number of gods and just worship the Sun God under the name of Aten, but many ordinary people felt deprived of their household gods and Tutankhamun gained popularity and favour with Osiris, it was said, by restoring the old religion. This led to the change of his name. Amun was the King of the Gods and TutankhAMUN became the name of the boy who had originally been called TutankhATEN. The British originally, at the finding of his tomb in 1922, spelt his name TutankhAMEN, but the final 'E' was changed to 'U' by the time of his great London Exhibition in 1972, although TutankhAMON also seems to be acceptable. In hieroglyphics there are no vowels, hence both 'E' and 'O' have been used. AMUN, it seems, is preferable to show the renewed worship of AMUN.

Was it regrettable that Akhenaten's changes were not accepted? He might have founded an early monotheism.

As we reached Tutankhamun's tomb, we shared in some of the suspense that Carter experienced. It was an awesome moment as the guide led us in. The entrance was bare and at first forbidding, but soon we were in a kind of picture gallery with Egyptian life unrolled before us on the walls. The King is seen sacrificing, seen wearing the head-dress of Osiris, the god of the after-life. The Sun God is there in his barque that crosses the heavens every day, people bring gifts, food, flowers. The blue lotus is the favourite.

I might have said more about the boats of Egypt. Boats belong to the gods, the pharaohs, the traders and the ferrymen – crossing the heavens, the underworld or just the Nile.

I might also have included one other queen, the last of the queens of Egypt, Cleopatra. She did not conquer her enemies, but she knew how to conquer hearts. She may not have defeated Rome, but she defeated two Roman warriors – Antony and Caesar. I leave it to Shakespeare to describe the boat she rode in, a queen aspiring to be a goddess.

Sketch on papyrus of a lady applying lipstick.
Probably a bronze mirror C 1300 BC.

Cosmetics had an early start! Cleopatra knew all about aids to beauty!

The barge she sat in, like a burnish'd throne,
Burn'd on the water: the poop was beaten gold;
Purple the sails and so perfumed that
The winds were love-sick with them; the oars were silver,
Which to the tune of flutes kept stroke, and made
The water which they beat to follow faster,
As amorous of their strokes, for her own person,
It beggar'd all description; she did lie
In her pavilion – cloth of gold of tissue – ....
On each side her
Stood pretty dimpled boys, like smiling cupids,
With divers colour'd fans...

Poetry of passion. Magnificence – or vulgar decadence? The long greatness of Egypt succumbs to Rome, as the man of Rome succumbs to the woman of Egypt.

Ancient Egypt occupied most of our time, but we also did a little sight-seeing in Cairo, visiting mosques and marvelling at the forest of minarets. We also saw the souk and the famous Shepherds' Hotel, once the paradise of the famous and of army officers in war time. We had tea in the famous Groppi's, the ladies rendezvous for teas and coffees, and we bought new shoes, as we had been advised that Cairo was the place for shoes. We had walked so much that I think we really needed replacement footwear. We also saw and liked the old Anglican Cathedral, shortly to be demolished to make way for a new road.

The old All Saints' Cathedral

The new All Saints' Cathedral

If you go to Cairo, do not miss the Coptic Museum. Although Arabs are the natives of Egypt now and Islam is dominant, the Copts can claim more truly, I believe, to be the descendants of the Egyptians of the past. Their churches and their art are well worth seeing wherever you may come across them.

One of the joys of travel is meeting different people from different places and different backgrounds and doing different things. One can make mini-friendships, lasting perhaps only a few hours. In Luxor, I met someone who added greatly to my understanding and appreciation of ancient civilisations. He was a Classics Don at Cambridge, disguised as an Army Major for the time being. His knowledge of the Greek and Roman civilisations gave him a special approach to the Egyptian world and he was eager to see how the one had influenced the other. He was a most interesting and stimulating companion on several of our visits; just one of those people who can add much to one's pleasure – and knowledge in his case – in a very short time.

Cairo, City of Minarets and Mosques

P.S. to Haifa – Two More Visits Made From There

I ought to mention Tel Aviv, where you will probably land if you travel to Israel by plane, developed out of a district of Jaffa in 1909, when immigrants from Russia settled there. This area was given the name Tel-Aviv, which means Hill of Spring, in 1910. The State of Israel was declared by Ben Gurion in the Mayor's House, in Tel-Aviv in 1948.

Under the Mandate, Jaffa (the Beautiful) was regarded as Arab and Tel-Aviv, Jewish. Israel has made them one, Tel-Aviv-Jaffa (Yafo). I did not find either of them beautiful, but did not know either well. I visited a hospital in Tel-Aviv when one of my girls had an accident on her bicycle and was suffering from concussion. I would trust their medical services. Not so long ago, a friend had a heart attack on the plane to Israel. I think her only problem with their health service was the difficulty of understanding one another. In my time, English was so widely spoken that I think the language difficulty is a recent development.

I had several pleasant visits to Jaffa, staying at the Mission schools. My most interesting memory was visiting Caesarea from there. It was a dead city then. We bathed there; good, clean warm water. Now it has been wonderfully excavated.

We recalled its great history, going back to the time of the Phoenicians, but named Caesarea by Herod the Great, to honour the Emperor Augustus. Jews and non-Jews lived in the city he created with a temple, a hippodrome, a theatre, a thriving harbour and good water supply. It became, under Rome, the residence of its Procurators, including Pontius Pilate. Here, St. Peter baptised the centurion Cornelius – the first baptism of a non-Jew. St. Paul was a prisoner here for two years.

Jewish risings took place and were suppressed. Later, a strong Christian community developed and there was a Bishop of Caesarea. In the 7th century, the Arabs took over until 1101, when the Crusaders got the upper hand, but the Muslims again seized power and Turkish rule dominated till the Mandate years of Britain. In 1940, the Jews set up a nearby Kibbutz. Since Israel began its rule, they have much credit for the wonderful archaeological work of restoration that they have done. Now, in the 1990's, Caesarea is something of a resort.

Aqueduct, at Caesarea.

And here I will say my farewell to Haifa. I had enjoyed being there; very glad I had not missed getting to know colleagues and some delightful girls, a few still my friends now that they are grandmothers and I in my nineties! I was ready to go home to see my parents, perhaps to link up again with University friends, get experience in British schools and look to a different future. I left in December, 1945.

I travelled with another member of the Jerusalem Girls' College staff (Dorothy Norman, who had previously been in Haifa) on what was now a semi troop ship – in a cabin for six (occupied by us and another lady and her two daughters). We were on board for Christmas. Our one ordained man, a Methodist, took our Christmas Services. Dorothy, a Vicar's daughter, had some hesitation then about taking Methodist communion, but I had none. I thought of my dear old grandfather setting off to Chapel on Sunday mornings in sombre black and chimney-pot hat, with Bible and prayer-book under his arm. His hair and beard were white, his eyes gleaming blue and his smile gentle – a saintly, faithful Methodist.

Postscript

From time to time, I have been asked two questions: 'Have you ever been back?' and 'Would you like to go back?'

To the first I answer, 'No'. My husband never wanted to go back, preferring to remember the Holy Land as he knew it. After fighting in North Africa in the desert and then having a spell in hospital, he had been posted to Intelligence in Jerusalem, where he found peacefulness and rest and happy days – and he found me!

I understood his point of view; sometimes shared it, knowing that not all changes would be to my liking. Ever since we were married we have, almost without exception, travelled together: I never wanted to go without him. I also know that majority opinion says, 'Going back never works!'

But I often like to defy majority opinion. Would I like to go back now, in my nineties? In many ways, the answer is 'Yes'. I would like to see the agricultural and horticultural changes the Israelis have made. In photographs now, I see a land graced by trees that were not there when I was. I would like to see the excellent museums that have increased and the wonderful excavations that have revealed so much. I would love to see the restored Caesarea. If anything could have turned me into an archaeologist, it was Caesarea. Whenever I went there, my fingers itched to scrabble in the sand and bring to light so much historical treasure that was then half-hidden. Masada and Qumraan were undiscovered in my day – well worth returning for.

Farther afield, I would like to reach my near misses – Gerash, Palmyra, Petra. To these I would add Persepolis and perhaps Baghdad and parts of Turkey, especially Lake Vann, with its beautiful swimming cats. I always wanted to visit Persia too, but politics have brought associated dangers that restrict travel today.

If I were based in Jerusalem, I would like to attend again some Russian Orthodox services; I would go to the Church of St. Mary in Gethsemane. Other times, perhaps, some gentle donkey would let me ride him in the desert. It would be lovely to see the desert 'blossom like the rose'. I would like to burst a Dead Sea apple and scatter its dust; I would even like to uproot a mandrake and hear it squeal! – only I would probably do the squealing. I would probably content myself with looking at the beautifully designed arrangement of its mauve flowers.

The young see visions; the old dream dreams!

Now, as is appropriate for old age, I travel vicariously, I travel first class but second hand, I have armchair comfort with a good book to read; I share other people's memories and go where they have gone.

As you know by now, I love to quote – I have so many literary friends whom I know from their writings. My last quotation is with apologies to Stevie Smith – I hope you end with a smile:

> *"I believe tremendously in the significance of age;*
> *I believe that a writer is wise at 50,*
> *Ten years wiser at 60, at 70 a sage..."*

What of 83 to 84? Wiser more and more? I leave it to you to say! Writing as this book goes into publication: what is expected at 95?!

Just once more, I must indulge my love of quotation.

At the end of his book "From an Antique Land", Julian Huxley wrote:

> *"It is one of the duties and privileges of man to testify to his experience, to bear witness to the wonder and variety of the world in which he finds himself. I had the fortunate experience of being plunged into the Middle East and its history; and in this book, I have tried to give my personal testimony of the impression which that experience made upon me. I am only too well aware that my acquaintance was brief and my experience superficial. But the impressions it made were profound, as well as vivid; and the attempt to order them into communicable form has been a satisfying, though sometimes a difficult task."*

These words express exactly my own final thoughts.

❖ ❖ ❖

End Piece

I wish to express my thanks to all who have made this book possible:

- Mr Nicholas Kilpatrick (my lawyer), who suggested publication and has helped throughout.

- Mrs Liz Berretti for help in 'book-making' over many years, especially now with the illustrations.

- Mr Edward Sutherland for photographs taken recently in Israel.

- Finally, I wish to thank my publishers for all their detailed work and help.

I am now 96 and wish all my readers pleasure in reading of work overseas in the last years of British Rule. I hope the Golden Ball and the Golden String will draw you into sunshine and pleasure such as I had.